MW01077520

OPUS ANGLICANUM

OPUS ANGLICANUM

A practical guide

Tanya Bentham

CROWOOD

First published in 2021 by
The Crowood Press Ltd
Ramsbury, Marlborough
Wiltshire SN8 2HR

enquiries@crowood.com
www.crowood.com

© Tanya Bentham 2021

All rights reserved. No part of this publication may be reproduced or transmitted in any
form or by any means, electronic or mechanical, including photocopy, recording, or any
information storage and retrieval system, without permission in writing from the publishers.

British Library Cataloguing-in-Publication Data
A catalogue record for this book is available from the British Library.

ISBN 978 1 78500 896 2

Cover design: Peggy & Co Design
Photography: Dr G Davies

Acknowledgements
I would like to thank Brenda Scarman, Mary Frost, Anna Novitsky, Amanda Ashton,
Liz Elliot, Kathleen Griffiths, Dr Timothy Dawson, Hazel Johnson and Bess Chilver
for their input to this book.

Typeset by Peggy & Co Design
Printed and bound in India by Parksons Graphics Pvt. Ltd., Mumbai.

❧ CONTENTS ❧

Introduction   7

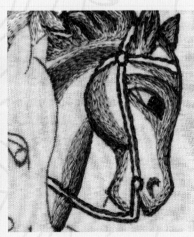

INTRODUCTION

Essentially, opus anglicanum uses just two stitches – split stitch and underside couching – so it must be pretty straightforward, right?

Not really.

Opus anglicanum is as much an artistic style as it is a form of needlework. It is a style that affects everything, from the choice of the original inspiration that forms the basis of your design, to the selection of materials, right down to the placement of each individual stitch.

It is slow, too, so, if you need a quick fix, go to do some cross stitch; if you want to get your teeth into something, try opus.

Even in its secular forms, all medieval art addresses the divine, and opus anglicanum is no exception. It plays with light in much the same way as the great Gothic cathedrals do, by manipulating the light to create something that is more than the mere sum of its parts. The reflection of light on the filament silk and gold threads that are used for working opus anglicanum is as important as the stitches themselves, and I hope to show you how to play with light, as well as how to perform two very simple stitches.

It is not my intention to provide a history of the technique, but inevitably history will be mentioned, because it affects the design choices made throughout this book. The book will deal only with the early period of opus before the Black Death changed the technique into a more debased style and faster form of needlework.

This is a guide for getting on with things, and, if you start at the very beginning, you can use it as a complete course for a beginner, or you can dip in and out of it if you already feel more confident as an embroiderer. Every project is chosen to showcase at least one new variation of the basic technique, with each project increasing in difficulty throughout the book.

CHAPTER 1

MATERIALS, TOOLS AND FRAMES

FABRIC

The fabric that I have used throughout this book for the examples and projects is a fine ramie canvas. Ramie is a plant fibre similar to linen, and the two corresponding fabrics would often be lumped together historically. I use ramie because it is finer than any linen that I have been able to find in repeatable quality. It is about 80 count, and I use two layers, which I usually machine-stitch together around the edges of the pieces before attaching the seamed, double-layer fabric on to the frame.

When working opus, you make a lot of holes in the canvas, so, the finer its count, the less these holes show. The results of opus are best if you never split the individual threads of the canvas, so, the finer the canvas is, the less chance there is of it being damaged.

Where a coloured canvas is used, I have used a twill silk similar to that seen for historical examples, backed with two layers of my usual ramie.

THREADS

For opus anglicanum, it is essential to use silk threads – and in particular filament-silk threads – for working split stitch, which forms the majority of the stitching of an embroidered piece. There are exceptions to this, for example, when working couching with metal or metal-effect threads, and linen thread is also needed for couching. Cotton threads should not be used, as explained further in Chapter 2.

This is a close-up of a single layer of the ramie fabric used for the examples and projects throughout this book. The translucency of this fabric is apparent.

We will explore the characteristics and uses of various silk thread types and other thread types in Chapter 2 and subsequent chapters.

TOOLS

I don't use many fancy tools and materials: the following items are about all that I need, in addition to the silk thread for stitching and the fabric upon which to stitch.

Some people like to use a magnifier when working opus, but, to be honest, I find that a good light source is of more use. Get something bright that can be directed to where you need to see.

Transferring designs

The ramie that I use is quite translucent: if you photocopy your design and hold it against the back of the fabric (prop this fabric–photocopy sandwich up against the pages of a thick book or two, so that the fabric is pressed against the design), you can trace the design lines easily. You can

Marking designs

When it comes to marking designs on canvas, I like to use something that won't wash out or fade. Most opus projects will take much longer to work than a fade-out pencil will last for, and wash-out markers are a bit pointless, because, once you have put the gold thread into your project, it is not the best idea to wash it. I prefer the permanent pens intended for fabric that you can buy in haberdashery shops, although some people swear by the kind that you buy in art shops: whichever you use, do a quick wash test first, just in case of surprises.

Graphite pencil is a bad idea as a marking medium and tool, because it tends to rub and can leave your threads looking grubby, especially if you are working with pale colours.

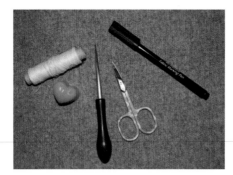

These are the main tools that I need for working opus (from left to right): good linen thread; beeswax, for conditioning the linen thread; a stiletto, for making holes in things, especially the canvas, and for poking; small scissors (I don't buy expensive ones, just lots of pairs of brightly coloured, cheap ones); and a permanent fabric-marking pen.

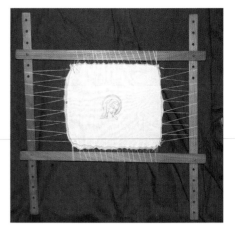

Here you can see a typical slate frame, bearing a laced piece of fabric with a transferred design.

get really good A4 LED light boxes quite cheaply, which are great for tracing, and some people insist on taping the design and overlying fabric to a window for tracing. I always prefer to have the fabric laced on to the frame before transferring the design; this way, the canvas can't move around under the pen, and you get a more accurate drawing.

The prick-and-pounce technique is really only practical if you want to work a particular design more than once, or if you have repeated elements, otherwise it is an awful lot of work for something that you want to mark only once. I have always suspected that professional medieval workshops kept a selection of stock designs, and probably complicated shapes like the lobed quatrefoils used in the Syon Cope, marked out on vellum for prick and pounce but that more-bespoke designs were done as a one-off and always drawn freehand.

FRAMES

Embroidery hoop

I don't recommend using a hoop for opus. Not only were there no hoops in the medieval period but also they really don't keep enough tension for the technique, plus it is very difficult to get canvas squared within a round thing.

Slate frame

This is the most authentic medieval type of frame to work on, and they are still widely available today, often combined with a set of trestles on which to rest them. You can get really good tension on these frames. I tend to use my slate frame mostly when doing medieval demonstrations, because the big disadvantage of a slate frame and trestles is the amount of space that they take up: it is really best if you get the trestles positioned the way you like them and leave them undisturbed, which isn't always practical in a modern home.

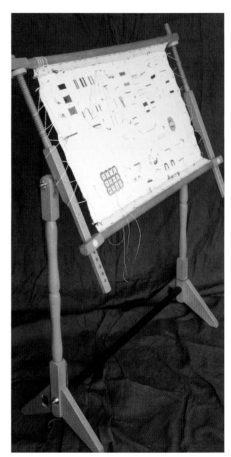

This is a typical floor frame, set up ready for working some more embroidery.

The other disadvantage that I find to this type of frame is that I constantly lose the pegs that hold these frames together, and so I end up holding mine together with snapped-off bits of dowels and pencils or giving homemade biscuits to the nearest woodworker in exchange for freshly carved pegs.

Floor frame

I prefer this type of frame when working at home. It holds great tension and folds flat against the wall in an instant, so it is much easier to clear away than a slate frame and its trestles. This type of frame is also ideal if, like me, you prefer to work with your frame at a 45-degree angle: this allows me to sit on the comfy sofa and lean my frame back into my lap. I admit to having six of these: some of them are over thirty years old and still work fine, so I can vouch for the fact that they are worth the £50 or £60 investment.

You set up this type of frame in pretty much the same way as you do a slate frame, sewing the fabric to the top and then firmly lacing along each side, but it is important to buy the type that has a big screw at the side, as for the featured frame: it allows you to increase the tension easily.

You sometimes find floor-standing frames with a rotating bar that is tightened by a metal wing nut, which doesn't hold tension at all.

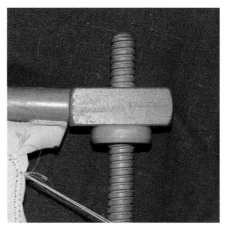

Here you can see the tightening mechanism of a typical floor frame (such as the one pictured earlier). This mechanism effectively holds the set tension of the fabric.

Small frame

A cheap option for beginners is to get your nearest friendly woodworker to make a simple square or rectangle slightly larger than your canvas – you can even use a chunky wooden picture frame with the glass and pins taken out as an improvised frame. This is the type of frame that I use when teaching classes, and they work quite well as long as you tighten the lacing properly.

If I have to work on a small frame without trestles, I find that it is still far less irritating to use than is a traditional slate frame, because a small frame doesn't have bits sticking out.

This is how a small frame looks with a properly laced-on canvas, ready for work.

LACING

Anchor the canvas by passing the lacing thread around one corner of the frame, then spiral lace along one side. Now, pull each loop of the lacing thread as tight as you can. Lace the opposite side of the canvas to the frame and tighten as before, then work back and forth between the two sides to achieve even tension.

Lacing thread

Whichever type of frame you use, a good, strong thread for lacing the sides of the canvas is essential. The medieval option would be a thick linen thread, but I mostly use a cotton thread, DMC Perle 5 (also commonly labelled Coton Perle or Pearl Cotton); they sell this thread for crochet under the name DMC Petra 5, which works out very cheaply compared to the little skeins sold for embroidery.

The disadvantage of a linen lacing is that it will stretch with high humidity, so you have to constantly relace your frame. In contrast, cotton thread isn't as affected by atmospheric humidity.

CHAPTER 2

OPUS STITCHING

Although opus anglicanum sometimes includes small areas of other stitches for effect and texture – laid-and-couched work, trellis couching and even tiny areas of satin stitch turn up from time to time – there are two stitches that define this style of embroidery: split stitch and underside couching. However, simply mastering these two stitches is not enough to make something opus.

Split stitch is used like a paintbrush, with every stitch being carefully placed and its direction being carefully chosen to express shape, light and character. Unlike later techniques such as crewel work, where the stitcher must show mastery of dozens of different stitches, opus is about knowing every subtle nuance of only the two simple techniques of split stitching and underside couching. Split stitch is covered in depth in this chapter; for an introduction to and instructions for, underside couching, *see* Chapter 6.

THREAD CHOICE AND CHARACTERISTICS

As introduced in the previous chapter, the stitching thread used for split stitching absolutely must be silk – and not just any old silk but filament silk: it reflects the light and plays with it to create three dimensions out of two.

Filament is silk reeled directly from a cocoon, as one long, continuous fibre only. This fibre is barely visible to the naked eye, so often several are layered into one thread for stitching with. Generally speaking, throughout this book, four strands are used for the stitching of drapery and other background details such as floors, but only two are used for the faces, and this echoes the practice used for original pieces.

Layered filaments can then be twisted to make the plied threads that most of us are used to, such as the Como silk that I use from time to time. Such twisted filaments are distinguished by their high lustre; they can be used as they are, or sometimes, as with Como, I pick them apart to use as filament threads.

Most of the silk currently available, however, is spun silk, which has a rougher, duller appearance. A true filament silk comes from the traditional Chinese method of production wherein the silkworm is never allowed to hatch and eat its way out of the cocoon; because the hatching process would break the filament, instead, the worm is boiled inside the cocoon and one continuous filament is able to be reeled off. Spun silk is made either from broken filaments or from cocoons where the silkworm has been allowed to hatch and eat its way out of the cocoon, thus breaking the filament apart in the process. If you pull apart the individual plies of a spun-silk thread and try to sew with them, they will break because they are much weaker, being made of many short broken pieces of silk filament.

Filament silk is flighty stuff. I often tell students that this is the naughty child of embroidery threads. If it can find a way to misbehave, it will: it will snag on the slightest thing and tangle if you so much as look at it funnily. There are fierce debates about whether or not to use thread conditioners with filament, the main argument against being that they dull the shine. I don't use conditioner on my thread, but I think it is a good tool for a beginner to use. Think of a thread conditioner as the training wheels that stabilize a small child's bike – they are something really useful for your first baby steps, but you want to get rid of them as soon as possible, because you will look rather silly if you keep using them into your teens.

The best way to make sure that filament silk behaves is a bit of self care. File your nails. Use a hand scrub once a week to slough off rough skin. Moisturize. Then moisturize again. I am very keen on a solid hand-cream bar that I keep in my sewing box that is made from beeswax and cocoa butter, because it goes on quite dry and doesn't make the threads sticky if you use it on your hands and then embroider straight away.

Como silk

This is a filament silk that has been twisted and is sold as ten- and twenty-five-gram cones for weaving and as spools. I use this for many different things, and it can be pulled apart into four or sixteen strands and then used for embroidery. It can be used whole for underside couching or making decorative braids for edging and finishing.

Woad-dyed silk from The Mulberry Dyer

This thread is now sadly discontinued. It is not quite as shiny as some of the other filament silks, but it has more body and sits on the canvas more like the original silks do.

Spun silk

This is made from broken silk-filament fibres and so is less shiny. I keep two weights of this in stock: 60/2nm, which

Seven different types of silk, from left to right: Como silk thread, woad-dyed silk thread, spun-silk thread, DeVere Yarns 36 thread, DeVere Yarns 60 thread, tram silk thread and DeVere Yarns 6 thread.

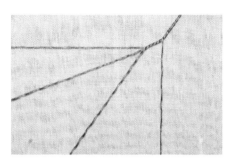

This is Como silk deconstructed into four constituent strands. Each of these can be split into a further four smaller strands.

is roughly of the same thickness as sewing cotton, and 30/2nm, which is thicker – the spun-silk thread in the earlier photo is of the 30/2nm weight, which I bought undyed and dyed myself by using woad.

This spun-silk thread is used for stem stitch and the upper layer of trellis couching, where it provides textural contrast to the shine of filament silk (see the 'Trellis couching' box in Chapter 12), and for assembling finished projects (see Chapter 16). However, it is not used for working split stitch in opus anglicanum.

DeVere Yarns 36 thread

This is another twisted-filament thread. I don't use this much: it is of a similar weight to 60/2nm thread but a lot more expensive – you would use them both in much the same way for working opus anglicanum.

DeVere Yarns 60 thread

This is a very loosely twisted filament, basically ten threads of their 6-count thread. This is interchangeable with the DeVere Yarns 6 thread, if you want to be lazy (which I very often do); you can pull a strand of this 60-count thread apart and have five two-thread strands ready to sew with without having to mess around.

Tram silk

This is also sold for weaving as ten-gram cones or spools of 500 metres in length. It comes in a far more limited range of colours, but it is cheap and sews up quite nicely. It is slightly thicker than DeVere Yarns 6 thread, which makes the tram silk thread easier for beginners and for experimenting with. The limited range of colours isn't really a problem; in fact, it encourages a more medieval way of working, as medieval embroiderers didn't have hundreds of colours to choose from. When working on your own medieval designs, it is actually very freeing to limit your colour palette, as it saves time agonizing over which of thirty shades of blue to use.

DeVere Yarns 6 thread

This is a very fine, flat filament. Normally, you would use at least two strands of this

A reminder about thread type

You will achieve the full effect of opus anglicanum only if you use filament silk; even spun silk won't bring out the full beauty of the technique, and, if you use cotton thread, it won't be opus at all.

At the top is a row of split stitch worked with filament silk, in the middle with DMC stranded cotton and, at the bottom, with spun silk.

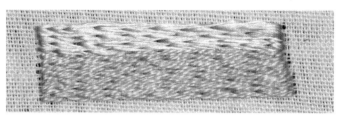

These two threads are pretty much the same of shade of blue; however, not only is the texture of the cotton (bottom) rough but also, as you can see, all the light is visible in the silk (top) – the cotton is dull, dead stuff by comparison.

held together. One strand of sewing thread should be of roughly the same thickness as one thread pulled from the background canvas, so two strands is the minimum that I would use with the fine ramie that I prefer as canvas. One strand is almost too fine to see and doesn't give significantly better results. In practice, two strands held together are used for flesh and at least four for drapery, in line with original practice, where the flesh is always treated with more detail than the clothing.

WORKING AN OPUS ANGLICANUM PIECE

General points before you start

⇛ You need to stitch with filament silks in order to achieve the full effect of opus anglicanum; any other thread type won't match the characteristics of true opus.

⇛ Pack your stitches closely together, then pack them even closer. If you look at an area that you are trying to fill with split stitch and think 'Yes, I just need one more row to fill that', you almost certainly need two, or possibly three.

⇛ Always split something. I will remind you of this so often that you will feel like you are a teenager again and your mum is nagging you to pick up your socks/close the door/do your homework. This repetition is because this point is so important.

⇛ Never be ashamed when you realize that you left a tiny gap in your stitching; go back and fix it by adding a few extra stitches as needed. But, when you do go back, always fill the gap by bringing the needle up through and down into – or splitting out of and into, respectively – the existing stitching and following the direction of the original stitches.

⇛ Be aware that going back and adding just one stitch can change the whole expression of a face: it is definitely worth doing this sometimes, to achieve the desired effect.

⇛ The initial drawing that you transfer on to your canvas is only a guideline. If you later think that the hand should be positioned at a different angle, change it. If you draw the line a bit wobbly, smooth over it when you stitch, and, if you want to sew an angel in a cowboy hat, well, yee-haw!

⇛ The colours used in original pieces and other examples of opus are again for reference only and don't have to be replicated. Angels can have pink hair if you want them to. I recently taught an online class where each student worked the same angel, but each angel had individual hair and varied

wings, and it was wonderful to see all of the variations.

⇛ Use an exfoliating hand scrub before working with filament silk. This thread will snag on the tiniest roughness on your skin that you didn't even realize was there before, and, although moisturizing will soften the rough skin, it won't remove it.

⇛ Get rid of any rough edges on your nails before starting to stitch.

⇛ Moisturize often!

⇛ Take regular breaks. Opus requires mental alertness and concentration: you have to think about where you are putting each stitch and how it will affect the outcome. I never sit and sew for more than an hour without getting up and moving around a little bit. This break-taking is especially important when it comes to working underside couching, which can be very hard on the hands.

Notice how much light is bouncing off the top row of stitches in comparison to that of the bottom two rows in the accompanying

If you have a range of ten shades of blue, from the palest to the darkest, such as those shown here, choose ones that will contrast.

Here, I have picked out the second, third, and fourth shades from the original range. They tone beautifully, but they clearly don't contrast.

Here, I have picked out the second, sixth and tenth shades. There is a stark contrast between the light and the dark shades, with a medium shade in the middle.

photo. With opus anglicanum, it is the light that is important: essentially, we are going to play with the light and manipulate the way that it bounces off of the filament silk. Opus anglicanum plays with light. Silk filament brings the light to your stitching in a way that no other thread can match.

The contrast is even more obvious when you see a block of silk filament worked right up against one of cotton, as demonstrated in the next photo.

Colour

I have used DeVere Yarns and tram silk threads throughout this book, but you can easily swap these to use Pipers Silks or Au Ver à Soie or any other brand, just as long as the thread is of a reeled, flat, filament silk. It just has to be shiny!

Don't be afraid to swap the colours used for the examples and change them at will, and don't worry about matching the shades that I have chosen exactly – choose something that looks about right, and shade numbers be damned.

One thing that I will emphasize is not to use too many colours. It is all too easy to fall for temptation and buy all of the colours available and then try to use them all at once, like an over-excited child in a sweet shop, but medieval embroidery tends to have a limited palette. Choose three or four shades of each colour and use them throughout the same piece. Buy all the colours if you must (and, let's face it, we all want all the colours, because they are shiny and pretty and the possession of a complete set of something makes our little monkey brains happy), but please use them on different projects.

When depicting drapery or other shapes in opus, don't fall into the modern trap of being tasteful. Opus needs contrast.

To illustrate the point about the importance of contrast, if you use the three shades shown above for your three layers of colour within a piece of drapery, you might as well do the whole thing as one flat blob of colour, because there isn't enough contrast between the lightest and the darkest shades in order to distinguish between the stitches of the different shades.

There is no real subtlety in the next selection shown above right, but this is the combination to choose for opus, because it will show off all of the work that you put into shaping the drapery.

THE BASIC STITCH: SPLIT STITCH

The basic split stitch is very simple to work.

I will repeat to the point of nagging that you must always split something. The first split made is the splitting of the previous stitch.

It is important to note that the third stitch should come up right next to the end of the first stitch and halfway along the second stitch, so that the whole row of stitches maintains the same width and body. To continue the row of stitching, every new stitch made splits the previous stitch made halfway along its length.

The end result can easily be mistaken for a row of delicate chain stitch. (If you ever do public demos, you will get sick of people explaining to you that you are doing chain stitch.)

I am not one to obsess over the appearance of the back of a piece of embroidery. Original pieces are often messy, and they do have knots, at the back. As the appearance of the front of your work improves, the truth is that the back will get neater as well, but if all you ever worry about is the back then you are focusing on the wrong part of the embroidery.

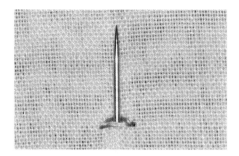

Bring the threaded needle out from the back of the canvas to the front of the work, and make a straight stitch about 4mm (just over ⅛in) long by taking the needle back down into the canvas, to the back of the work. With the needle, come up again halfway along the first stitch, splitting this stitch in two (as shown), hence the name, split stitch.

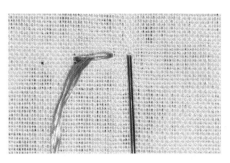

The next stitch made should be of the same length as the first, but half of it should overlap the first stitch, so that each stitch advances by only half a stitch.

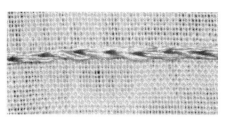

The aim is to have a smooth, even strand of stitches in a row.

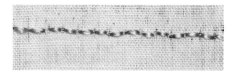

On the back of the work, this is what a properly worked single row of split stitch should look like.

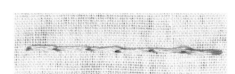

If you compare this stretched-out example with the previous front-of-work one, you can see how lumpy the row has become – thick where the stitch threads overlap and thin and straggly where they don't.

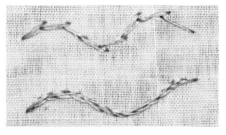

Here you can compare the top row of stretched-out split stitch with the neat row of properly done stitches at the bottom.

Basically, if the back of your split-stitch rows starts to look like this, you are doing the split stitching wrong.

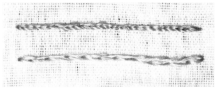

Shown at the top is a row of split stitches that are worked very small, with each stitch covering only one or two threads of the background canvas, and shown at the bottom is a row worked with each stitch covering between eight and ten threads of canvas (exactly how many depends on how fine your canvas is; for the examples in this book, I am using a fabric of roughly 80 count throughout).

The back of an embroidery

Knowing what a stitch ought to look like at the back of the work is an important aspect of understanding how the stitch is constructed, and split stitch is no exception. I struggled with split stitch for years, until it occurred to me that split stitch is actually the very same backstitch that I was taught for stitching straight seams when I was a child – but upside down!

If you turn the fabric over to look at a row of split stitch, the rear should pretty much look like common or garden backstitch. It doesn't have to be the world's neatest backstitch: it can be a bit wobbly, but, if you aim to have most of the stitches joining up with one another, the front will by default look pretty good too.

Opus anglicanum is a slow technique, and there is a very real temptation to try to speed up the process by stretching the stitches to make them go further. By this, I mean going only a canvas-thread distance or two back into the previous stitch, instead of halfway back along that stitch.

The resulting straggly effect is bad enough on a straight row, but, if you start trying to work around a curve, it becomes spiky very quickly.

Size matters! A common problem that I see is people making their stitches too small, as on the top row of the accompanying photo – the size of the stitches of the bottom row is about the optimum stitch length.

You need a stitch as tiny as those shown on the top row only when you are working faces or going around a tight curve (as the stitch needs to compensate for the angle of the curve); most of the time, you need to work your split stitches to the size shown for the bottom row. If you work all of your stitches too small, two things will happen:
- ⁊ You will never finish your embroidery.
- ⁊ The look of the stitching will change. Notice how much darker the top row

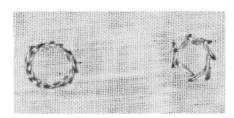

On the left is a circle of tiny stitches; on the right is a circle of the same size but worked with fewer, normal-length stitches. For the right-hand circle, you can see how the normal-size stitches – which are too big for this purpose – make the circle spiky and irregular – the stitching line is no longer smooth, and the circle looks more like a polygon.

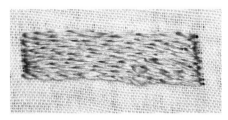

If you look at the side of this block of stitching, you will see that the rows are never more than two threads of the background canvas apart – I usually aim for one, but this canvas is very fine.

looks. Both rows have been worked with the exact same strand of silk, but the shorter stitches of the top row change how the light bounces off of the silk. You need some length to the stitch to optimize the play of light, just not too much length: it is a delicate balance.

When you do need to go small with your stitches is when you are working circles and tight bends.

Rarely in opus anglicanum will you use a single row of split stitch standing alone. Normally the rows of stitching are packed very closely and tightly together, to the extent that sometimes you may wonder if you have added anything at all.

The silk does spread out a little along its width, but you shouldn't rely on that to fill the space, especially if the finished piece will move in any way, as gaps can open up between the rows of stitching when the fabric bends.

You must pack your stitches tightly. Don't worry if you sew over the previous row a little bit when working the current row.

Snags

As I said earlier, filament silk sometimes feels like it is actively trying to find a way to misbehave, and snags are common, even when you have remembered to moisturize beforehand. If you notice a snag straight away, you can fix it there and then by pulling the excess thread through from the back.

However, quite often you won't notice a snag until you are stitching the next row or you are several stitches along – this is fine thread being used and, if the light is at the wrong angle, it can become invisible.

You do not have to pick out the entire row to fix one snag within it.

If you unpick every time that you miss a snag, you will never finish your embroidery. Luckily, this is where those tightly packed rows work to your advantage. This is also one of those instances that demonstrate that expertise is not about never making a mistake but is about knowing how to fix those mistakes when you inevitably make them.

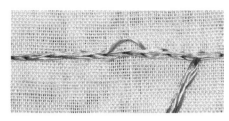

This is how a snag might look on the front of the work; you should always keep an eye open for snags cropping up while you stitch.

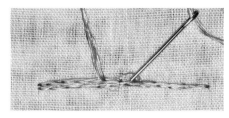

When you are working the row alongside that containing the snag, make sure that you pull the snag loop to one side and sew it down as part of working the adjacent stitching of the current row.

Once you have worked the next few rows, you won't even be able to see where the snag was.

On the left is a curve worked so that each row is quite separate and distinct from the previous row; as you can see, the rows start to lean away from one another, and gaps are appearing. This will get even worse if the embroidery will be on an item that will move when in use.

On the right is a series of curved rows worked really closely together. Each of these two samples is of just three rows of stitching, but you can see at once how much thinner the arch is when the stitches are properly packed, as on the right.

In this example, I have worked an exaggerated, expanded version with three thread colours to show you how the packing of stitches works on a curve. Notice how each row 'bites' into the previous one, effectively knitting them together.

Curves

As mentioned previously, your stitches should get smaller when working curves and tight circles, but they should also get closer together. Pay attention to how you pack the stitches around a curve, otherwise things can look messy very quickly. Remember that this is not a technique in which you can cheat and speed things up by working fewer stitches.

Really, the technique of working a curve properly comes back to me nagging you to always split something – here, you need to split into the adjacent row to achieve proper coverage of stitches over the canvas.

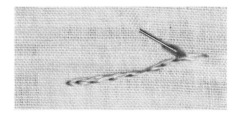

To achieve a good point, work your row of split stitch just a millimetre or two past where you want the point to be, then bring the needle up and out through the fabric and split the previous stitch as usual, but, instead of taking the new stitch forwards in line with the rest of the row, go in the opposite direction to change the stitching angle as necessary.

Points

Whereas you can work around a soft curve, there are many folds in drapery that need a sharper look. The principle is the same as for biting into a curve, but you do it at only one specific place, to form the point.

As you continue to fill up the point with stitching, make sure that you split the tip of each subsequent row into the one before, to maintain the sharpness of the point. By overlapping the rows of stitching slightly, you will keep the point clean and sharp. I have worked this example with two colours of thread so that you can see this effect clearly.

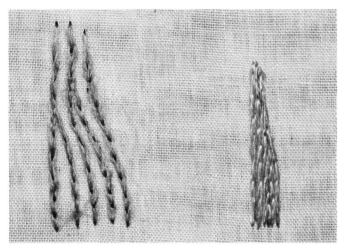

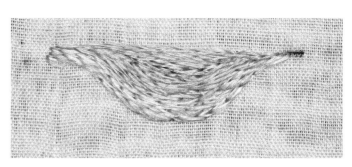

Here, I have worked an expanded version on the left, with larger gaps between the rows of stitching as usual, so that you can see the rows splitting into one another, and a two-coloured version on the right, so that you can see how the tightly packed stitches begin to flare out.

As shown in this image, you can fill by working your rows one beside the other until the narrow areas are filled (the cream stitches) and then continue to fill by working the stitches in a continuous spiral pattern (the blue stitches). This is a perfectly acceptable way to fill, but it can create two visually distinct areas in the silk, because the stitches of the two areas lie in different directions and therefore interact with the light differently.

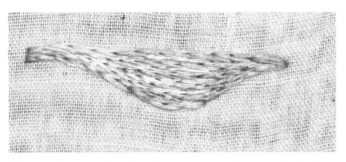

When working such layering with one colour, all you need to do to work the next row is to carry the thread across the back of the work to split out of the row that you have just worked.

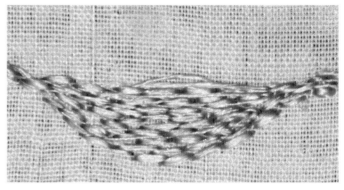

When working this type of layering, don't worry about the long threads travelling across the back of the work; your subsequent rows will stitch them down – you can't even see them here.

Layering

Often, you will want to widen an area of solid colour without turning around a point. You can achieve this by layering.

Instead of working the next row of stitching along the full length of the previous one, work it only part way and then split the end of the final stitch into the previous row.

Work the next row along the full length of the area being stitched, then make another partial row and then again work the next row along the full length. This will gently flare the area of stitching.

This is a really useful and important technique that I will come back to time and time again, but it is just another variation on the principle of always splitting something.

The layering technique offers an additional way of filling large areas, as shown in the accompanying photo.

Alternatively, you can fill an area by using layering with interlocking rows of stitches, as shown here, with two colours. You can even work a gentle outward curve with this technique.

Unpicking

I rarely unpick split stitch, and, on the whole, I advise against it. Because you split each stitch, you are essentially destroying the thread as you go along, and, if you

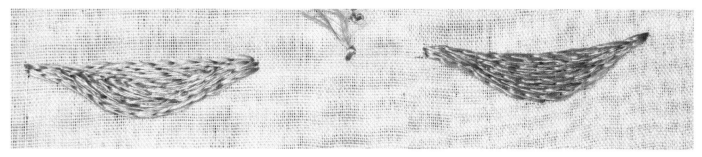

As you can see from these side-by-side samples, each technique gives you a different texture, because of the way that the light plays on the stitching. On the left is a spiral filling; on the right is a layered filling. Both are useful in different ways.

have packed the stitches properly, it can be almost impossible to see where one row of stitching ends and another begins. Trying to unpick a row that is snug against another can easily and quickly result in wholesale destruction.

As long as your stitches are properly packed, you can cover even stitches worked in a strong colour contrast, and the threads are so fine that there's no discernible textural change where the new thread is worked over the old. This is one of the few instances where silk filament can be helpful and forgiving.

Once you sew over it, it will disappear.

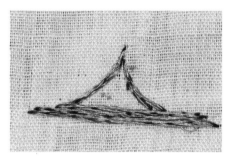

I normally choose to work over small errors instead of picking them out, as shown here. It is quicker to achieve the desired result and far less soul-destroying.

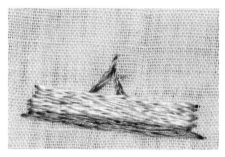

You can see here that I have worked over part of the grey point shape shown in the previous image with a much paler thread, masking it completely.

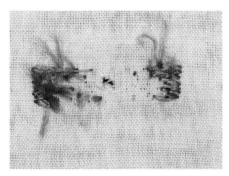

More than once I have seen students try to unpick a patch of split stitch at home and end up with a hole in the canvas. It is all too easily done: either you pull too hard or try to cut out a stitch and slip, in each case resulting in that unwanted hole. However, all is not lost – small holes within an area of split stitch can be patched.

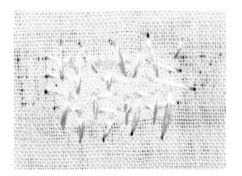

Take a single layer of the same cloth that you are using for your canvas, lay it over the hole, and the use a silk thread to darn it thoroughly into place. Essentially, you just have to go back and forth with running stitch in both directions to make a rough grid, as shown. It doesn't have to be pretty!

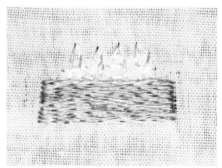

Once you sew over it, the added cloth and the hole beneath it will disappear.

CHAPTER 3

TECHNIQUES FOR FACES, HAIR AND HANDS: BIG ED AND LITTLE ED

Faces are the most difficult and technical part of any composition in opus anglicanum, and they are crucial because so much of the mood of the composition depends upon each face being just right.

A lot of the expression of the face comes from subtle changes of direction in the stitches used to form them, and from the play of light upon these stitches, and all of this relies heavily on the use of filament silk. Using the same techniques with cotton, even though the thread is almost as fine, will always look clunky and amateurish by comparison, because cotton is dead and dull next to the light that plays upon silk.

Filament silk is hard enough to see at times, let alone photograph, so I have decided to work this demonstration face twice, as Big Ed and Little Ed, with the normal two strands of DeVere Yarns silk, with the stitches densely packed and smoothly finished, as opus anglicanum should be worked, and with a broken-down strand of Como silk at a much larger scale, to show the placement and direction of each stitch, respectively. For the larger face, Big Ed, I have expanded the stitches so that you can clearly see the path of each line of stitching. The two faces have been photographed side by side at every stage. Please note that the lines on the Big Ed head are intended as a guide: they indicate the direction and flow of the lines for the little brother, Little Ed, but the number of lines is not necessarily the same and should not be taken as for a counted pattern. The rows of the stitches for the little head should be packed as closely and as tightly as possible. Think of the Big Ed head as a contour map or expanded diagram.

Every face in opus anglicanum is slightly different, so I will also provide step-by-step photographs for the face, or faces, of each project throughout the book, so that you can learn and adapt your own technique for the other projects as well.

I have chosen a wise-looking saintly type, from a panel held in the Metropolitan Museum of Art in New York, in the three-quarter profile most common to opus, but I have also worked a few atypical faces that I will discuss at the end of this chapter. I am not presenting step-by-step photographs of the atypical faces, but I will provide tracing and contour drawings as a basis for you to experiment further.

THREE-QUARTER FACE

Step-by-Step Instructions

1 The first step is to trace the drawing twice on to the canvas; once at actual size, for Little Ed, and once at a large size, for Big Ed.

As you can see here, I have enlarged the drawing so that my study head (left) is about four times the size of the original head (right), so the details of the stitching really should be clear enough to everybody to fully understand how the stitches have been worked.

2 Always begin an opus anglicanum face with the outline of the eyes, nose and mouth, including the ears where applicable. How much of these edges you outline depends upon the angle of the face and the amount of hair the individual has and any headgear that they are wearing.

The nose is nearly always connected to the brow of the eye that sits furthest from the viewer, and the profile of the nose itself and this connecting line also provide some of the structure of the face. The mouth, like that of an emoji, is rarely anything more than a line, and often this line is disapprovingly downturned, or it is sometimes just a befuddled little slit. Teeth are shown only on evildoers.

The eyes and mouth are the main things of importance for any face – think of the iconic smiley face, where the human face is boiled down to two dots and a curved line: it is still instantly recognizable as a face because the core elements are present. By placing and shaping these elements correctly, we not only define the face but also provide the frame from which the face's flesh will hang.

3 The eyes are the most important element of every face – get these wrong and the whole thing – the face, and potentially the composition – goes squiffy. Facial symmetry is an important part of beauty and still applies to a face seen in three-quarter profile. If you are drafting your own pattern, make sure that you can draw a ruler-straight line from the corner of the left eye, directly through the dead centre of the pupil, and onwards to the corner and pupil of the right eye, because, if the eyes aren't level, the face will look wrong, possibly stupid, probably deranged and almost certainly a little bit disturbing. Wonky eyes are a top tip if you want to portray a lunatic, though.

The pupils in opus are always exaggeratedly large, and care should be taken to fill the area of the eye properly. Normally, only one row of colour is needed for the iris.

One point that I will reiterate over and over again to the point of nagging is to always split something. Blending the rows of stitching together to make a block of flowing colour is important, and you should aim to never be able to pick out one individual stitch from the mass.

4 The face now becomes a series of geometric shapes fitted around the frame that we have just established. Think of the way that Picasso created a face from dissonant shapes huddled together, or of the way that Maori facial tattoos follow the contours of the flesh – we are going to do something similar, but we are going to blend the shapes more smoothly, so that they eventually hang as one face.

One of the most prominent pieces of geometry in any face is the cheek, so I always start with that.

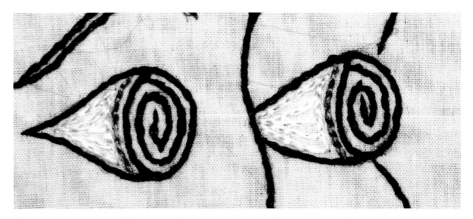

The point of always splitting something applies also to the eyes, so notice how my row of white starts in the corner of the eye and skims the edge of the iris before skipping back to the corner, and then a whole new row is split out of the first and heads towards the iris again – splitting each row down into the row that edges the iris adds to the continuity. All of the stitches worked in the white thread flow in the direction of the gaze, splitting out from one point of origin, so that, in the correctly sized version, they become a single area of white that suggests the shape of the eye.

With many of the other faces in this book, I will emphasize that the cheek should be a firm, high and round apple, to create the appearance of youth, as demonstrated in the accompanying Welsh queen piece by Brenda Scarman, one of my students, but the wise man we are stitching overleaf is a bit of a saggy old codger, so his cheeks are more oval than round, instantly giving him a more aged look.

In this case, you can see that I have placed my first stitch on the corner of the man's beard, but it could have come out of the corner of his ear.

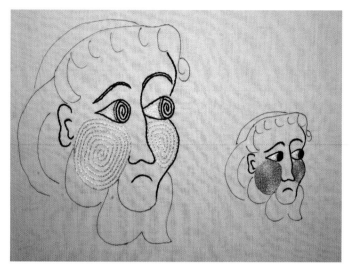

The right-hand-side cheek as we look at the face is smaller, because of the perspective of the turned face, so it should be stitched as a smaller oval. The shape of this cheek will be even more irregular, but it should still be filled with the same inward-turning spiral.

Whether presented as a firm, youthful apple or a saggy, old oval, the cheek is worked as a continuous spiral of stitches.

Wherever possible, the shape of the cheek should graze the lower edge of the eye and the side of the nose, in order to join the face together. For an older face, the shape will fill the entire region of the cheek, but, with a younger face, the higher cheekbones will leave the jawline area empty, to later be filled as a separate shape.

Always begin the spiral on the outer edge of the circle or oval when working a cheek; if you begin in the middle, its far more difficult to get the placement correct. Spiral around in ever decreasing circles until you reach the centre, where the final stitch should be split back into the previous row.

5 Often, I move on to working the forehead next, but this chap has such emphatic eyebrows and such an expressive nose that I am going to deal with those now, including the outer ears. Other than placing the main outline and the cheeks first, because they define so much of the face's character, there really isn't a strict order to do things. I tend to do forehead, then nose, then chin as a matter of habit, and, after practice, you may find that you have a different order of preference.

If you run your finger over your own face, there is a definite line that runs from the top of the ear, under the brow and down to the tip of your nose (even if you have a few wrinkles acting as speed bumps along the way, the line is still there): it is this line that we are going to track with stitches.

Notice that, where the width of the area to be filled varies, I have added discrete extra rows of stitches along the way, splitting them into and out of the other rows at each end by using the layering technique illustrated in Chapter 2, about basic split stitch. Rather than wait until I have lots of long rows filling most of the space and then filling in the extra gaps at the end, I have anticipated the variations in space and blended the short extra rows in between the longer ones, so that they are better blended with the rest.

At this stage, every single row is split into or out of another; there are no blunt ends to any of the rows. Avoid blunt ends for any row of stitching, because they are visually jarring.

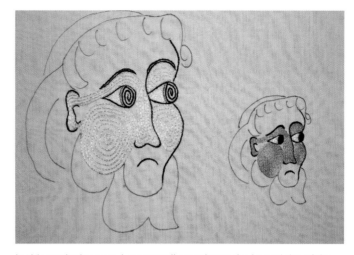

In this particular case, I am actually starting at the lower lobe of the ear and following it around to the top, before stitching under the brow, so that the face ends up joined together more effectively.

All of the rows flow from the starting point at the lower earlobe and end at the side of the nose, where they are split into the cheek shape, but one final row (note that for the smaller face, this is several rows, densely packed) loops back up to fill the space between the length of the nose and the cheek, creating a subtle shadow and adding shape.

The right underbrow is filled by working from left to right, splitting each row out of and into the outline first row of stitches that hugs the underside of the brow.

6 I am going to do this man's chin next. A pert, female face will have a much less pronounced muzzle than that of this old coot: this makes this wise man great to practice with, because he doesn't need to be treated with any subtlety. His heavy chin just adds to his hangdog, jowly expression.

I have begun by splitting out of the cheek, near the point of his beard, and spiralling right around his lower face to emphasize his nasolabial lines. I keep this spiral going until it touches one side of his mouth, after which I work a smaller spiral around the lower part of his chin. This leaves part of his upper lip unfilled (on the left-hand side as we look at the face), so I finish up by adding a couple of lines that are split out of, and then into, the other rows and which flow in the same direction.

7 The forehead is next and is relatively simple to work.

As with the underbrow, I have used contour lines split into and out of the main ones to blend the irregularities of the shape, especially between the brows. I have introduced the contour lines relatively early, but, if you add them later, the frown will deepen.

I worked all of the forehead lines from left to right, but you could try working blocks of three or four lines right to left with stitches slightly closer together, to give the effect of wrinkles via a subtle change in texture, resulting from how the light will interact with these stitches.

I have begun my first line just above the ear and connecting to the brow: on both faces, this is a single line, placed to avoid having an unsightly kink if I had started this stitching further up.

The first line hugs the brow, dipping down between the brows to give this face a little frown. With many faces, especially female and younger faces, I would trace a straight line across the gap between the brows to avoid any hint of a frown, but old saggy chops here hasn't been keeping up with his Botox, so this frown is an important part of his expression.

The next line starts at the left-hand side, up in the hair, and slides down the side of his face before joining up with the first line. I also put a line down the opposite side of the face, and these vertical lines will give the horizontal filling lines something to bite out of and into – both will be pretty much obscured once the forehead is filled.

8 Whether or not you use a dark outline for the bald spot on top of this man's head is a personal choice – on the whole, I prefer not to, as I think that the darker outline throws the head too far forwards, whereas going without adds more of a sense of perspective. His bald bit is worked as a series of curved lines to fill the space.

In this case, I haven't tried to split anything when working this part of the head but have instead finished each row of stitching with a blunt end – however, each of these ends is below his hairline and so will eventually get covered up. Each row will therefore still be split, but split into.

9 The last step in filling in the flesh is to go around and fill in all of the small connecting areas. In reality, as you gain experience, you will find yourself doing this as you go along, but I have done it last for demonstration purposes.

In many cases, such as below the eye and at the corner of the nose, all that is needed is a tiny triangular shape worked in split stitch to join the larger geometric shapes together smoothly. I often refer to these areas of triangular filling as being worked with triangular stitching. In other places, you will need to add a whole line, as you can see that I have done at the side of the eyebrow, and the join will blend most smoothly if you follow the direction of the existing stitches.

Notice again that even these tiny areas of stitching split into and out of the larger areas.

Having now filled in most of the little spaces, the biggest area still to fill is to the side of the ear. Often ears are hidden by hair or headwear, so you won't always have to embroider them – which is probably for the best, since ears are tricky things to draw at the best of times. Here, I have split out from the oval of the cheek and looped around the inner ear before going across under the brow. If you run a finger along the side of your face, you will see that this part of the ear is very much a continuation of the cheek, and all I have done is follow this with stitches.

HAIR

10 Sometimes I work the hair first, sometimes last; it mainly depends upon my mood, because faces are more difficult than hair and, some days, I don't feel up to it, so I do the hair first! This time, I have done the hair last.

When you do the hair last, you should split the rows of stitching out from the flesh where the follicles would be. When you do it first, you should cover the origin of the hair with the outer row of the flesh colour, to blend these elements of the head together.

Nevertheless, there are exceptions to every rule. In this case, although the top of the hair should connect to the flesh by either splitting out of or being covered by it, the ends of the hair don't have to be split and can stand independently, just like the end of a real strand of hair. However, in order to give a well-groomed appearance, it is best to clump the ends of the hair into locks.

Hair colour in opus is not always realistic: blues and greens are quite common. Females tend to have more realistically coloured hair, often some variation on Teutonic blonde, which was considered the most desirable hair colour throughout the Middles Ages (some things never change). It is often men, especially older men, who have more unusually coloured hair. Sometimes, as with the gaggle of balding wise men on the Metropolitan Museum fragment, it may be a case of using many colours to distinguish one head from another, but I think a lot of the blue rinses are meant to represent grey hair. Grey is a surprisingly tricky colour to achieve with natural dyes, so the obvious choice would be to use blue instead, and it is a conflation that the modern world still uses – when I picked up my cat Branston from his mum, I said how pleased I was to get a grey kitten, only for the very nice Maine Coon breeder to tell me firmly that he is blue, not grey.

It can be very tempting to stitch all of the dark lines in the hair and beard first and then come back later to stitch the lighter colour as a second stage, but this is not the best way to approach working of the hair. Very few people are accurate enough in their stitching to leave a perfectly even gap between two lines, especially not when stitching the often tousled lines that hair demands. Add to this the fact that, even within one proprietary range of threads, you often find dramatic differences between the thread thicknesses of two colours, there are clearly just too many variables. In fact, while stitching the hair for the smaller head, I found that the darker-grey thread was so much finer than was the pale blue that I switched to using six strands instead of four to even out the widths.

The best way to work the hair is by layering the colours one strand at a time – in the case of most opus hair, one strand of hair is worked with two rows of stitching (for Big Ed, one hair strand represents two rows). Some hair is depicted as a strand of one colour and three of another, but two by two is by far the most common approach. One to one turns out to be far too delicate to give the bold striping that is such a distinctive mark of the hairdos of opus anglicanum.

There are two basic ways to approach this use of two colours of thread. One is to keep two needles in play – one for each colour – to layer first one strand and then the next, parking the unused thread when not in use. This method builds up the hair from a single point until all of it is completed, and this allows for an even alternation of colour.

However, I tend to find this method a little problematic, mainly because of the flighty nature of filament silk: it is just too easy to catch the parked thread and end up with a horrible, fluffy mess. I prefer to divide the hair into sections and then to work several areas at once, using one colour at a time. Most opus hair divides quite easily into clumps; in this case, you have got two distinct sections of the beard below the chin, another section of beard at the cheek, two curls and a straighter bit to one the side of the head, and three curls and a quiff across the forehead.

I began by splitting out of his chin with four strands of dark grey and working down to the bottom of the left beard, and then I did the same for his right beard. I then worked a row on the side of his face – this used up one needleful of thread. I then repeated this entire process by using a needleful of the paler colour, continuing by alternating needlefuls of colour until the hair was completed, and by moving on to the adjacent section of hair as soon as the first was full. Because you have several sections on the go at once, this method can sometimes feel like you are not making as much progress as usual, then it suddenly all comes together at once.

I always try to work the hair out from the flesh, rather than the other way around, because it feels – and ultimately looks – more natural that way, as if you are growing the hair out from the flesh.

Hair is one aspect of opus where you really don't need to stick religiously to the original drawing. It is better to just go with the flow and play with the curls and contours – and I have been known to give angels a Mohican before now.

Hairdos

These three angels and one queen were all worked by students of one of my courses. By changing the colour and styling of the hair of the original image, each student has made the resulting embroidery their own.

DIFFERENT FACES

Straight-on profile

11 This example is worked entirely with tram silks, which are great for practising with. Two threads are used for working the face and four for the hair.

Although a face with a straight-on profile is not as common as the three-quarter-profile face, there are quite a lot of full-frontal faces in opus anglicanum. They tend not to be ordinary citizens but are usually saints, angels, or Christ, as shown here, although there are occasional oafish characters shown with frontal faces, as the style lends itself quite readily to an idiotic expression.

One of the big difficulties with a frontal face in any medium is the nose, and in opus it is usually indicated by two lines on each side of the face's centre line and by a detached tip. In this case, his long nose makes him sombre and a little bit pompous.

As with any other face, I began with the cheeks, which in this case are quite high, with a saggy jaw below, but it is the exaggerated muzzle that really finishes his dour look here. In some ways, it was actually easier to connect the areas of this face together than it would be with the more conventional three-quarter profile, as all of the lines of stitching spiral symmetrically out from the cheeks. Take care to make the cheeks as symmetrical as possible, though, lest it looks like he has befallen an unfortunate medical incident.

This face is based on the John of Thanet Panel, showing Christ in majesty, in the Victoria and Albert Museum (V&A) collection, London.

The hair on the original is very pale blonde; the hair of my version is much more yellow, but I have emphasized the yellow by paring a double strand of it with only one of brown, thus allowing the golden tones to come to the fore.

I have mentioned before that the drawing should only ever be a guide, and, in this case, you can clearly see that I have roughly sketched the hair to begin with, then just worked outwards from the temple until the covering of hair reached a sufficiently bouffant character.

Side profile

12 I worked this example entirely in split-down Como silks, using one-quarter of a quarter strand for working his skin and a full quarter for the hair. I love the copper colour for a Mediterranean complexion.

The face was worked in a very similar way to the dominant facet of a three-quarter-profile face, again beginning at the cheek. In this case, the spiral of the cheek is worked out from the original central circle until the curves become part of the underbrow area, which in its turn curves back to become part of the forehead.

The muzzle area was also worked as a unit, but, instead of going around and around as for the previous figure, his lips are worked outwards as two shapes, capable of delivering a kiss.

His nose was perhaps the easiest of all the faces in this chapter to work, partly because it is so big and partly because it integrates into the face so well.

Three-quarter profile, especially for undesirables

13 You may well be thinking how hideous this man is, and he is meant to be – that is the point. Everything about this face tells you instantly that this character is a wrong'un as deftly as the big, black Stetson in a cowboy movie.

His skin is not only worked in two colours instead of the usual one but one of the colours is a deeply unnatural blue. Shades of a rotting corpse, blues and greens, are often favoured for such faces. You may think this is hammering the point home

This profile face is from the same Metropolitan Museum panel as that of the two Eds, and it shows Judas delivering the fatal kiss to Jesus. Because of the kiss, Judas is by far the most commonly depicted profile face.

in a less than subtle manner, but remember that most people in medieval times would not have had the opportunity to see these pieces in the close-up detail that we are used to today. The copes and albs upon which opus was first mounted were brought out on high days and holidays only and would have been glimpsed in passing over the shoulders of the crowd, so such instant signifiers were an important part of the visual language of art. The same signs are also used in manuscripts and other medieval arts: they are not exclusive to opus anglicanum.

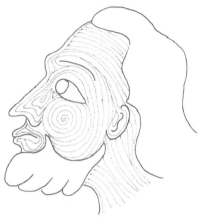

The ghastly blue–green flesh colours are mostly reserved for those who jeer and torture Christ, so they are often used for soldiers such as this one. The concept of historical accuracy was alien in the Middle Ages, so he is wearing a contemporary medieval style of helmet instead of anything remotely Roman.

Bared teeth are another sure sign of evil intent, but the face is more subtle than it first appears – the eyes are a little lopsided, with pupils smaller and beadier than the norm, and the cheek sags in an unusual teardrop shape.

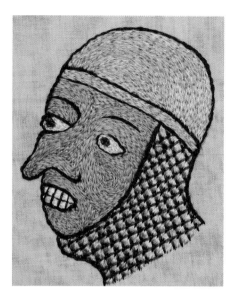

This little charmer is also from the same Metropolitan Museum panel as are Judas and the Eds.

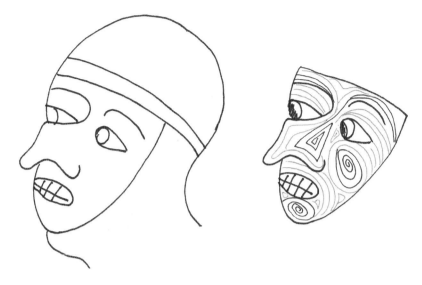

FEET AND HANDS

If you are like my mum and get freaked out by disembodied body parts, you might want to skip the rest of this chapter.

All of the hands and feet that I have used as sources for the following examples are from the Vatican Cope. I have used the same expansion technique as earlier to show the patterns of stitching on the most common shapes.

Feet

14 Feet are really easy! They are nearly always just filled by closely packed lines of stitching being worked down from the ankles.

Care is always taken to delineate each toe on a foot shown from the top, such as the one on the right-hand side; usually these types of feet are sticking out from under a robe, where only part of the foot is shown.

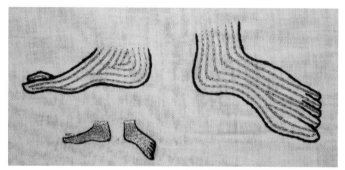

I have put in the weird toe on the profile foot on the left-hand side because I think that the Vatican Cope is the only place that I have noticed it: most opus pieces just show the side of the foot, with no detail at all.

As also for hands, feet should be worked with a finer thread than that used for the clothing.

Hands

15 Hands in opus anglicanum often display a series of standard gestures.

There is never any attempt to make the knuckles of an opus hand obey the physical laws of actual knuckles and bones, so don't worry if your stitched hands end up looking like an elegant bunch of chipolata sausages. However, they should be nice, long chipolatas, not stubby, little cocktail hotdogs.

I have no idea why the little finger on this type of hand often looks like an extra thumb, but sometimes it does.

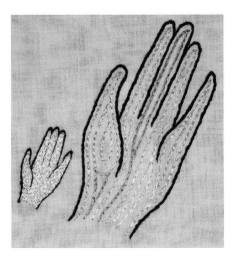

One of the standard gestures often seen is the palm thrown up, as shown here. When it is used for one of the hands of a person, it looks like a greeting, but often both hands are shown turned up like this in a gesture of amazement and dismay for figures viewing the crucifixion – it is meant to look solemn, but it always looks like medieval jazz hands to me.

The stitches of hands should flow out from the wrists in a manner reminiscent of the bones of a hand – think of an X-ray of fingers and hands and follow the same lines.

Given the religious nature of the majority of opus anglicanum, it should come as no surprise that the benediction, as shown in the accompanying photo, is a very common hand gesture.

Saints in opus anglicanum are often shown holding objects of martyrdom, and the evangelists are clearly recognizable by the gospels that they hold.

When the hand is cupped under the object that it holds, you normally don't have to depict all of the fingers, just a few of them fading to a point as they curl under the object. I think this is one of the easiest hands to do.

As for the previous holding example, when a hand is gripping something, you don't have to show all of the digits –

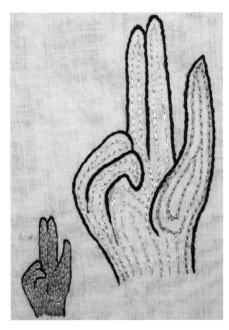

Here is an example of the benediction, which is worked in a similar way to the jazz hands, but with the two smallest fingers bent around together towards the palm. Working a spiral for the pad of the thumb gives extra depth to the hand.

sometimes the thumb is shown to balance the grip, but often it is simply omitted. The elegantly curling little finger is quite standard though.

Another form of grip is shown here, and I find this style particularly difficult to draw because it is so stylized. Although the stitches still flow in the same direction as the bones of a hand, there is something quite forced and mannered about this hand.

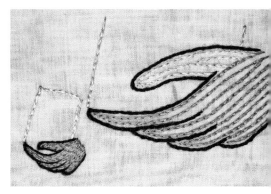

This hand is very similar to one of Rapunzel, who appears in Chapter 12.

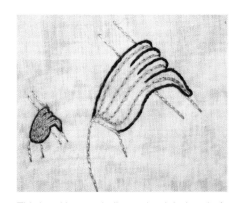

This hand is very similar to the right hand of St Michael featured the Syon Cope-inspired project in Chapter 7 that is being curled around a staff or spear.

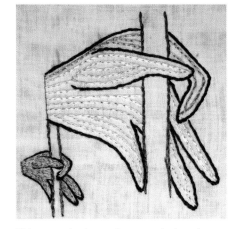

This example shows the opposite hand gripping a staff.

CHAPTER 4

Simple Shading and Surface Couching: The Riggisberg Lady

Techniques

Drapery, female face, simple shading, surface couching

This glamorous lady is based (with one small alteration) on an orphrey from Riggisberg, and she is thought to be of European manufacture in the English style. I have chosen her as the first full opus project for her elegance and simplicity, plus she does have rather glamorous hair. Despite her relatively primitive look, she actually dates from around AD1400, so she is probably provincial.

You spend a lot of time with these figures when you work on them; they start to assert their individual personality after a while.

Her drapery is very simple and straightforward, which is what makes her such an ideal starter project. We will be working her gown and cloak with just two colours each. Many opus pieces now appear to have been done with two colours, but it is mainly due to fading of the pigments

over time, and there would originally have been three. However, I always like to start students off with some two-colour shading, because it is a good learning exercise that helps you to think about light and shade. Often, if you are reproducing an existing piece, you have to do a certain amount of guesswork to use three or four colours, so starting with a more basic copy helps with overall understanding. We will move on to three colours in the next project, and, later still, we will look at more imaginative reconstructions using manuscript images.

STEP-BY-STEP INSTRUCTIONS

Materials

Fabrics

- Double layer of fine ramie or linen fabric (60 to 80 count), 10in × 12in
- Scrap of wool fabric or felt

Needle

- Size six crewel needle

Threads

- Silk-filament DeVere Yarns 6 thread, one 200m reel each in the following shades:
  - 01 white
  - 20 peach/pale pink
  - 44 black ebony
  - 51 sun/pale orange
  - 53 foil/silver
  - 55 beeswax/warm yellow
  - 79 moon/mid blue
  - 81 acorn/very dark brown
  - 112 dutch/dusty bluebell
  - 121 whiskey/soft brown
  - 183 bamboo/dirty green
  - 258 gimp/very dark grey
  - 266 fox/ginger brown
  - 321 ivy/mid green
    Please note that one whole reel of each colour is more than adequate for the working of this project: any thread remaining can be used for the working of several other projects.
- Gold thread, 1m (about 40in), either Japan gold or Benton & Johnson smooth passing of your preferred thickness
- Lacing thread

1 As usual, begin by transferring the design on to the canvas. With opus anglicanum, you are going to cover every inch of this drawing: any blank background space will either be covered by another stitch treatment such as underside couching (covered in depth in Chapter 6) or be cut away so that you can mount the figure as a slip (covered in depth in Chapter 15). This means that you don't have to worry about the background getting a bit grubby, nor do you have to worry if you suddenly decide that you want your lady to be holding a fluffy kitten or a small fire-breathing dragon instead of a box, because the drawing is only ever a guide and you can adjust it to your heart's content. To prove my point, I changed my mind after making my initial drawing and later gave her a frog to hold, who may well be a handsome prince. I am not good at resisting temptation.

2 Use four strands of gimp/very dark grey to outline the lady's clothes and hands, but don't worry about her face for now. Be sure not to flatten out that exaggerated thrust of the hip: this is a very fashionable medieval pose.

3 Use four strands of dutch/dusty bluebell for beginning to shade her cloak. The shading here is very simple, and all you have to do is follow the outline straight down from the shoulder. One reasonable length of thread will go pretty much from her shoulder to her ankle, but you can see that I have used the resulting end of each length to then work a line of shading for one of the shorter folds near the bottom of the garment, and this allows me to make the most of each strand. Wherever possible, split each line out of or into a previous one.

These blue shades would originally have been dyed with an extract of woad (*Isatis tinctoria*), which gives a much dustier blue than does the indigo dye we are used to today, so I have chosen shades that echo this characteristic.

4 Lady Riggisberg is quite a stiff little figure by opus standards, and her drapery reflects this, so I have just worked three rows of the same dark shade along each line of the cloak outline, including the bar across her throat, which represents the strap of her cloak. Notice that large areas of what looks like cloak are currently left blank; this is because these areas are where the lining is flipped back, so we will work them in a contrasting colour. Remember to split out of the darker colour and into it again wherever possible.

5 Fill in the rest of her cloak with moon/mid blue: there is much more of this shade than the darker shade, so this becomes the dominant colour of the cloak. Remember to follow the direction of the previous rows of stitching, splitting out of and into them so that the colours blend seamlessly.

7 Again, remember to split out of and into your previous stitches. Splitting into the previous row where a fold ends will allow the shape to come to a natural point and improve the flow of the drapery. If you just end four blunt rows side by side, as in the right-hand example, you will end up with an ugly lumpy bit of fabric instead.

Drapery lining

If at any point you think that you have crowded the lining with too much filling, you can re-emphasize the outline by adding more of the dark colour (grey, in this case) over the top. But be careful not to overdo it: use two strands instead of four, because, once your split stitch is properly packed together, it is almost impossible to unpick any single stitch without destroying several more.

So, use half of the original width of thread; you can always go over it twice if once isn't enough to achieve the desired result.

6 Her dress follows much the same pattern as for the cloak but is worked in different colours. This time, I have chosen orangey shades to reflect the widespread medieval use of madder dyes (made from extracts of *Rubia tinctorum*), as both of the thread shades used are similar to those extracted from the madder root. Reddish oranges are far more common in opus than what we think of as red today, because they were much cheaper to dye than a good deep red, for which imported *Kermes* insects (a European relative of cochineal that had already been exploited since ancient times) had to be used.

As with the cloak, work three or four rows of fox/ginger brown close to the grey outlines. Notice that, on the left of the figure, I have worked to the right of the lines, then, in the centre, I have swapped over to working to the left of each line, to round out the figure below the drapery.

Don't forget to work the ends of her sleeves where they peek out under her cloak!

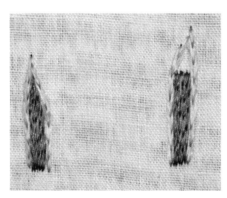

8 With the split-in, pointed example on the left, the next layer of colour flows smoothly around it, but, with the blunt example on the right, the second layer of colour is unable to flow smoothly, leaving a gap that will need to be filled later. The second, right-hand example is much more jarring on the eye: it makes you notice the stitches rather than letting you focus on the overall picture.

9 Fill the rest of her dress with sun/pale orange, with the stitches worked in the same direction as for the previous stitches and, as always, splitting in and out. Notice how the pointed ends of the dark colour allow the pale colour to skim and flow all around the inner shape.

You will need to use varying lengths of rows to fill her dress, remembering to pack the stitches very tightly together.

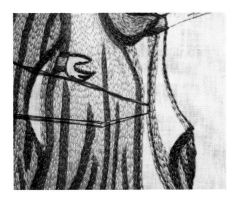

10 The cloak lining will be white but needs some shadowing to be added, and, for this, we are going to use foil/silver. You can shade white with any very pale colour, but a silvery grey is the best choice here, because it will tie in the lining to the blues of the cloak. If we shaded the lining with pale yellow or apricot, for instance, the lining would have a stronger visual link to the dress than to the cloak of which it is a part. Silver and blue are both colder shades, so they are read as one unit.

Try to use a light touch with the grey – work no more than three rows – as too much will make the lining look dirty.

Notice that I have flared out the grey shading where the swirl of the lining is wider by adding partial rows of grey carefully split out of the longer rows.

11 Begin adding the white of the lining by following the direction of the grey stitches and packing the rows tightly together. You will need to use the same technique of flaring out the rows for the white as you did for the grey in order to fill the shape smoothly. Remember that no individual stitch should stand out from the others: the aim is to hear the chorus, not a soloist.

12 Once the cloak lining is filled in, it should look nice and swishy. People think that wearing a cloak is about keeping warm: it isn't. Wearing a cloak is all about the swishing!

15 The frog's pupil fills the top half of his eyeball completely, since his eye is really too small to fill it with a circle. Use a spot of white for his eye, and then fill his body with three simple stripes of colour, each shaped at the ends to fit the curve of his outline. Bring ivy/mid green down from his nose and into his back leg, and use it for his front leg too. Bamboo/dirty green is used to add a small stripe along his side, and beeswax/warm yellow is used for his belly.

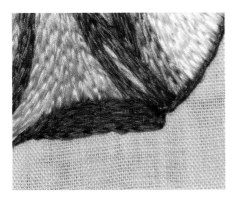

13 Medieval shoes aren't really glamorous, and there isn't much shaping that you can apply to a tiny toe sticking out from under a robe, so just fill in this shoe as a solid block with whiskey/warm brown.

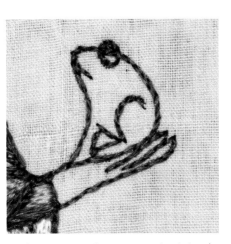

14 Go down to using two strands of gimp/very dark grey to outline the frog. Note that medieval frogs are very cartoonish: some don't even have front legs.

16 Going back to our lady, use four strands of black ebony to outline her face. It is not a complete outline, as the left side will be covered by the fall of her hair; work along just the right-hand side to define the cheek, then the nose and brows (work two rows for the brow). Don't worry about the line looking very heavy at this stage. As you can see when you fill the pupils and whites of her eyes, if you use the outline to split out of and into with your paler colours, they will soften and diminish this outline.

As I mentioned earlier for the cloak, you may even find that your subsequent work will almost obliterate this outline, so you might even want to go over it later and re-emphasize it. If you do, use only one or two strands, and take care – it is easier to add than it is to take away.

Normally the mouth in opus anglicanum is just a grumpy little brown or black line, but I often like to give my opus ladies a cheeky little stripe of pink lipstick, as here.

17 Often, I will do the hair after I have done the face, but faces are hard, and there are some days when you just don't feel up to doing anything difficult. Hair is always fun to do, especially princess-style, Duchess of Cambridge hair like this.

For flowing hair, I find it best to establish a dominant curl or wave first and then build on that. In this case, I stitched the flick of hair that flows down from the centre of her forehead and out to the side.

It is best to use two needles, one for each hair colour, at the same time, and just park the unused needle out of the way while you use the other one. Park the spare needle on the front of the canvas where you can see it, because, if you leave it at the back, it is all too easy to get in a tangle.

Often you can work two areas of the hair at once; you can see that here I have worked both the flick and the hair below concurrently. Once the flick was complete, I moved on to concentrate on the lower part.

18 Because our lady is in a conventional three-quarter profile, there is more hair on the left-hand side as we look at her than is on the right-hand side, and the hair on the right should be simpler, so that it doesn't distract from the direction of her gaze.

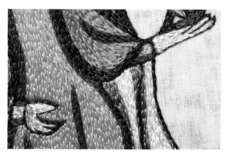

19 I have used a soft pink for the flesh. This isn't a conventional opus anglicanum flesh colour, as both sexes are normally shown with a pasty cream-coloured flesh. I am using pink here to show how subtle variations in colour can make opus look just ever-so-slightly not quite right. You are welcome to use a more traditional sallow tone here, but I wanted to show pink as an example.

Whichever skin tone you choose, go down to using two strands, and work the hands first. I always work the hands and feet before starting on the face, because, even if you have done quite a lot of opus, it can still take a moment or so to get used to the finer threads, and the hands and feet are less of a focus, so, if you are going to make a mistake, this is a better place to do so. Her hands are filled in very simple, linear stitching. As seen in Chapter 3, the stitching lines should flow from the wrist to the fingertips.

20 For the face, start with the apples of her cheeks. Her face is quite rounded, so there is room for a full circle of stitching on each cheek.

Because she is young and beautiful, you need to make sure that the apple fills as much of her upper cheek as possible, hitting the lower edge of the eye and the side of the nose. If you find it helpful, you can draw the circle in place before beginning to stitch.

Dragging the apple down and not hitting the lower edge of the eye, even by a fraction, will age her dramatically, as will making this cheek filling anything but a perfect circle, so go carefully.

21 Her forehead should also be smooth and unwrinkled. She hasn't kissed that frog yet, so her life is still carefree, and she doesn't have kids to worry about or a husband to drive her round the bend – those things are post-frog-kissing concerns.

Work her forehead by splitting out from the side of cheek and working up the side of the face. Keep the stitches completely straight across the forehead; don't dip between the brows: that would give her wrinkles.

22 Split out from the side of the forehead line, and work under the left-hand-side brow and down the nose until this area is filled. You can feel how continuous this line is by running a finger along your own face: you are basically following the line of the orbital socket of your skull into the cartilage of your nose.

Curl around the tip of the nose and split back into the side of the cheek to blend the flesh into one.

Your stitches will need to become smaller on the tight curves to keep them packed properly together. Try to split into the curves rather than creating distinct lines.

Fill under the other brow as well.

23 Because the apple of her cheek is quite high, she also has a distinct jawline. Split out of the apple again and follow the jawline down into the chin. Curl around the chin and up under the nose, following the shape of the nasolabial lines and spiralling around until the stitches begin to touch the sides of the mouth.

Fill the chin as a smaller spiral while echoing the larger spiral to fill the upper lip.

24 Finally fill all of the tiny gaps of the flesh of the face, remembering as you do so to split out of and into the other stitches, following the same stitching direction where possible and blending the stitches together.

25 Fill her neck on the diagonal. This stitching direction echoes both the line of the jaw and the line of the sinews in the neck.

SURFACE COUCHING

Surface couching, as the name implies, is simply the sewing down of a thread on to the surface of the fabric. Usually this technique is worked with a metal thread, as we are using here, but it is also sometimes used with silk outlines, as we will see for The Cherub project (*see* Chapter 7). It is one of those stitches that is used from time to time in early period opus, often for small details and outlines, but in later-period opus it is used to the exclusion of underside couching, because it is a lot quicker and easier to work.

It does have disadvantages though. A large area of surface couching lacks the flexibility of underside couching, and it is far more delicate, as it will easily catch and snag – an important consideration on items like copes, which are to be worn. Liturgical vestments had high status in the Middle Ages, but this doesn't always mean that the clergy treated them with care.

I am including a small project in surface couching as an introduction for those who perhaps haven't used metal threads before, as it is a good way to get used to the threads themselves before moving on to the more complex underside-couching technique, and also because I want to point out the way that the process of medieval surface couching differs from the standard, modern way of doing things.

Surface couching, whether ancient or modern, is merely a case of sewing down a metal thread by using a silk thread at regular intervals: that is pretty much it. You can sew down a single thread, or two threads at once. Two at once saves a lot of time, because the threads are so thin, and so is more usual than working with single threads.

The problem comes with the ends of the metal surface threads. These threads are created by wrapping a very thin strip of metal around a core of thread. Modern versions tend to use cotton, and medieval versions used silk; however, very early in the Middle Ages, the gold was wrapped around a single horsehair.

For modern goldwork embroidery, the threads are couched down with the ends remaining on the surface, and each row of couching has exposed ends, so you end up with a fringe of gold on each side of your work, for a while. Later, each of the ends is taken to the back of the work, by plunging them through the fabric.

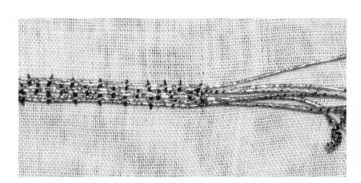

Often you sew with a silk that will tone with the metal thread – yellow for gold, white for silver, and so on, but I have used a contrasting colour here for demonstration purposes. As you can see, the silk is simply sewn over the gold surface thread at regular intervals, staggered in a brick-like pattern, being worked in the same position on every other row.

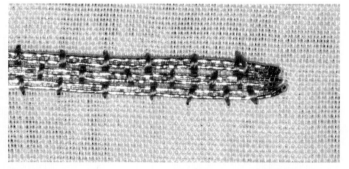

Modern passing threads are pretty tough, and, as the name suggests, you can pass them through canvas with care, as has been done here; the medieval versions (and indeed the modern Japanese versions and some vintage threads) are more delicate and will disintegrate if you try to sew with them conventionally. So, you don't sew with them, you sew them down instead, hence 'couching', which comes from the French *coucher* to lie. You make the metal threads lie on the surface of the embroidery. The trick is getting each thread to lie where you want it to.

Personally, all of those ends get on my nerves, and I constantly get them tangled up with the couching thread. But, personal feelings aside, the modern method makes no sense for medieval sewing, and you can clearly see in many original pieces that this was not how things were done – if you look around the edge of surface-couched pieces, you can clearly see the thread being bent back and kept on the surface, rather than being plunged at the end of each row.

Modern goldwork embroidery sometimes uses a passing thread with a percentage of gold, which is moderately expensive, but medieval embroiderers were using threads made from 24-carat gold or from gilded silver. Their gold threads were exponentially more expensive than those used by the average modern stitcher, and their embroidery was all about showing off, so why would you hide huge chunks of your expensive gold thread at the back, where no one would see it?

And, more to the point, why would your wealthy patron allow you to hide his wealth when he is paying you to display it? Every ounce of that gold was counted, and anything left unused would need to be accounted for.

So, for medieval goldwork, we don't plunge every end: we keep as much as possible on the surface where we can see it, because it is all about the bling, baby!

To finish surface couching the modern way, every single one of these ends must be plunged or passed through the canvas to the back of the work once the couching itself is completed, as has been done here.

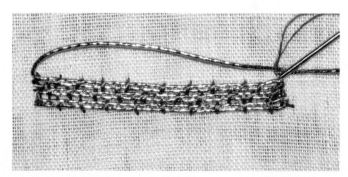

Here is an example of the correct medieval way to couch gold, by taking it back and forth across the surface, even when couching two threads at once.

You can see here that, in order to couch two surface threads at a time, I have to anchor the opposite end of the gold and loop it around – if your span of gold is very long, you can keep a second needle threaded to anchor the ends. Once I have the two threads lying side by side, I can couch them down as one, taking care not to let them twist around each other.

Depending on how stiff your gold thread is, you might need a small pair of flat, needle-nose pliers to pinch the thread ends and keep the folds tight.

Japan gold thread

I have used Japan gold thread for this project, rather than the passing used throughout the rest of the book. Japan gold thread tends to be softer than passing, so it is better to use for surface couching, because you can bend it easily around corners. If you were to use passing for this project, you may find that you would need to pinch the threads in the corners very tightly with pliers. Unlike the solid metal wrapping of passing, Japan gold has gilded-paper wrapped around the thread core; hence, it is much easier to bend.

Japan gold is more commonly sold in embroidery shops than smooth passing, and you can get it online from Midori Matsushima (*see* Suppliers at the end of this book).

26 I am going to apply our lady's surface-couched crown after I have applied her as a slip to some silk velvet, but because I don't want fibres of velvet poking through the gold (for more information about slips and how to mount them, *see* Chapter 15).

Having mounted the slip, I have sewn a small piece of yellow wool fabric where the crown will be – felt fabric is fine, but I tend to use scraps of wool fabric left over from costume projects, because this is a medieval way of doing things (and I actually am too mean to throw out tiny scraps of fabric).

It is best to layer a slightly larger piece of fabric than you think you need over the top of the head and where the crown will be and then trim it carefully to size before stitching it down, in case this fabric shifts a bit while you sew. Also, you get a much better idea of exactly how big you want it to be once it is properly in place.

The wool fabric present beneath the surface couching will also help to raise the goldwork to be at the same level as the stitching of the slip.

27 Work up from the forehead, couching two rows of gold at a time, as shown in the sample (though, you can couch just one row at a time if you find it easier). I have couched with the same yellow silk as used for the frog's belly, and I have kept the crown plain, but you could add jewels to her crown by couching small areas with a contrasting colour.

Continue working upwards until the yellow wool pad is mostly covered. As you can see, I have got an odd corner of fabric sticking out from under my surface couching, but I can trim that carefully away with sharp scissors – there is no need to worry about the rest of the pad coming loose, because it is well held down by the gold couching.

Don't cut and plunge the gold yet; we are later going to use the tail for the crown points.

28 One of the nice things about sewing directly on to velvet is that you can manage without having to draw a simple pattern. As you can see, I have marked where I want the crown points to be by running the tip of my needle against the grain of the velvet, to make a temporary scar. These marks won't last very long and will be easily removed by using a stiff brush, to brush the velvet's pile in such a way as to smooth its surface, but the marks lasts long enough for a small project such as this and will give enough of a guide to make the point symmetrical. Actually drawing on velvet with ink is a bit of a nightmare because of the way that the pile shifts, so I tend to avoid having to do it wherever possible.

It doesn't matter whether you work from the left or right at this point, so don't worry about which side the tail of gold thread ends up on. Just take the gold thread straight up from the end of your last row, couch it down along the line drawn in the velvet, curl the gold thread around at the top of the point and come straight back down.

29 Her crown is going to be of the classic fairy-tale variety, with three fleur-de-lys shapes along the upper band. Obviously, the fleurs-de-lys at the sides are in profile, so each has only one curl. Work straight back up the side of the point that you just made and then curl out with the gold thread about halfway up it. Fold the thread over at the tip of the curl and then work back down to the crown.

Once the gold thread is again at the body of the crown, work along the top of the crown shape until you reach the next place where you want to come up to stitch the next point, bearing in mind that the line that you have drawn into the velvet marks the centre of the point, so you need to create the first curl of the central fleur-de-lys a few millimetres before this mark, in order to make the point central.

30 For the central crown point, remember to work the other curl of the fleur-de-lys after the middle point, as this crown point, seen straight on, has a curl on both sides. It is a bit too small to draw these curls effectively on to the velvet when it come to the crown points, so measure each new curl against the one made before, to get them placed consistently.

She looks like a proper princess once she has her crown, but she still isn't sure about that frog...

CHAPTER 5

THREE-COLOUR SHADING: ST LAWRENCE

TECHNIQUES

Arcaded halo, drapery, three-colour shading

This figure is based on a fragment of opus anglicanum in the Victoria and Albert Museum (V&A), London, although I have given him back his feet, which the original is missing. I have chosen him as a starting project because I have always liked his little face; to me, he looks less like a saint and more like a very naughty boy who has just been caught scrumping apples – the expression on his face is adorable. So, although he is quite a simple figure, reproducing him contains the challenge of replicating a particular expression.

For this project, we are going to look at three-colour shading, rather than using the simpler two-coloured version as used for the Riggisberg Lady.

Step-by-Step Instructions

Materials

Fabric
- Double layer of fine ramie or linen fabric (60 to 80 count), 25cm × 30cm (about 10in × 12in)

Needle
- Size three crewel needle (I prefer a small crewel needle, for its slightly bigger eye)

Threads
- Silk-filament DeVere Yarns 6 thread, one 200m reel each in the following shades:
  - 01 white
  - 21 strawberry/pink
  - 38 parrot/pale blue
  - 44 black ebony
  - 47 bluebelle/dark blue
  - 53 foil/silver
  - 55 beeswax/warm yellow
  - 60 eggshell/pale brown
  - 87 conch/peach
  - 94 yolk/sunshine yellow
  - 111 regal/ purple
  - 112 dutch/smoky blue
  - 138 carrot/orange
  - 241 inky/ dark grey blue
  - 255 chilli/dark red
  - 266 fox/ginger brown
  - 321 ivy/mid green
  Please note that one whole reel of each colour is more than adequate for the work- ing of this project: any thread remaining can be used for the working of several other projects.
- Lacing thread

1 As usual, transfer the design on to the canvas.

2 Start by outlining his robe, collar and hands and the stones with which he is to be martyred. Use four strands of inky/dark grey blue thread.

‹**3** Work the dark areas of shading of the gown using bluebelle/dark blue. Keep this colour quite subtle: it is very easy to overdo the shading on drapery at the early stage. I have used only three, or sometimes four, rows of stitching on one or both sides of the outline, carefully following the same direction of stitching and packing the rows tightly.

4 When it comes to the branching of the folds, take care to split each row into the first to create a smooth point, and make sure to split out of the outline at the beginning of each row.

5 Add a shading layer of dutch/smoky blue next, again following the direction of the existing stitching and always splitting in and out. Notice that, at the top of the image, particularly on his sleeve near where his hand is raised, I have reduced shading with this colour to only one or two rows, but lower down, near his feet, I have built out this colour into a wedge, and, in some cases, even filled the area completely. This draws the light up to St Lawrence's face and adds perspective.

Drapery shading

How you arrange and execute the shading affects the overall look of the finished piece. All three of the test patches shown in the accompanying photo include the same three colours, but their proportions are different.

As with drawing, how you arrange the proportions of the different shades within a piece will affect the end look, and you can manipulate the shading to create a dark, rich look or a clean, bright one using the same set of colours. In practice, you may well use all three techniques for the same piece of drapery, using a dark arrangement towards the back and sides and a lighter one towards the centre, to round out the figure.

The patch on the left has two dark, four mid, six light, four mid and two dark lines of stitching. This creates a rounded tube or fold that tends towards the light.

The middle patch has six dark, four mid, two light, four mid and six dark lines of stitching. This creates a darker, richer fold.

The patch on the right has four dark, four mid, four light, four mid and four dark lines of stitching, to create a sharper fold with a more obvious direction of light.

6 It can be difficult to understand the point of following the direction of the existing stitching and carefully splitting in and out when you look at the piece flat on, but, if you tilt it, you will begin to see the way that the light plays upon the silk. The intended play of light is achieved by being aware of how the stitches are blended together.

7 Start filling in the rest of the robe with parrot/pale blue. The far-left fold as we look at the piece is fairly simple to fill, by just using repeated rows of stitching with a slight flare to accommodate the widening of the fabric towards the feet, but the two middle folds have to be worked carefully to a point, so remember to split into the previous stitching at the end of each row. With the more complex fold on the right-hand side, it is best to work alternately down each side of the fold until the two sides meet. If you work down one side only, the end result will look unbalanced. Working alternately down each side will leave small triangles of fabric left to fill later.

8 Continue to work down each side of the fold from the top. Split out from the apex of the top triangle and work downwards until you split into the bottom of it, then skip over the back of the work to come out at the top of the lower triangle. For this large lower triangle, continue the left-hand row of stitching down over the hem of the robe, to suggest the shape of the lower leg and foot below the fabric.

9 Once these folds of the fabric are all filled in, there should be a nice sense of depth to the robe.

10 Use foil/silver to add some shading to his collar and the inside of his robe cuff. I have used this pale grey to contrast with the blue of the robe, but you have to be careful: if you overdo it, the white of the collar and cuff will look grubby. Remember that you can shade white with just about any pale tone, and the colour you choose will affect the finished shade of white, so, for instance, blue will make it look cleaner, but yellow will make it look as though the wearer is a heavy smoker. Grey is unobtrusive until you use too much, so all you need is a hint, a line or two, to add a suggestion of depth.

Fill the brooch that fastens his robe with solid grey. If you wanted to get fancy, you could use metallic silver instead, but this is a beginner project so I am keeping it simple.

11 When the white of the collar and robe cuff is filled in, you should have just a gentle hint of grey remaining.

12 Only the cuffs of his under robe are visible, so it takes only a few stitches to fill them, and there is no point in trying to do anything complicated here. Use this stitching, worked with beeswax/warm yellow and fox/ginger brown for the cuffs, as a means to add shape to his forearm.

13 St Lawrence was martyred by being roasted upon a gridiron, so here he is presumably staring mournfully at the barbecue charcoal. Whichever interpretation you prefer, I have filled in what he is holding in his raised hand with chilli/dark red, strawberry/pink and conch/peach.

Haloes

There are countless variations on the theme of haloes in opus anglicanum. Some are filled with gold threads, some have a combination of gold and silk, some have pearls, and others are simply plain silk; I suspect that the choice had less to do with the whim of the stitcher than it did with the budget of the patron, gold thread being as expensive as it was.

At which stage you work the halo depends upon execution. A silk halo should be worked in sequence with the drapery and facial features, but a halo or any element featuring underside couching (see Chapter 6) is always worked last.

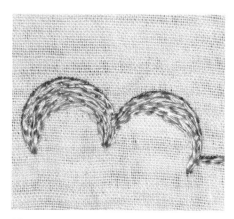

14 The original image that is the basis of this project has an arcaded halo of silk and gold, but I am adding an arcaded rainbow here for no other reason than that I happen to like rainbows, and since we are going to work a gold halo later in the book.

Begin at the outer edge of the halo, working a row or two of chilli/dark red before outlining the points and filling them in.

15 Carrot/orange is worked next. Each layer of colour should be of only two or three rows of stitching, so there will still be room for the other colours, but, in order to fill the arch efficiently, the colour at the apex of the arch needs to be thicker than that at the points.

16 In order to achieve this effect of the arcaded-rainbow halo, use the layering technique. Stitch about two-thirds of the way around the arch and then switch back and work to about one-third of the way around the arch (here, shown worked in two colours). The middle part of the arch will then thicken up, leaving the ends thin, so that there will ultimately be room for all of the colours. Remember to split the returning layer of stitching out of the existing one, in order to blend them.

17 Build up the layers of yolk/sunshine yellow, ivy/mid green, parrot/pale blue, regal/purple and strawberry/pink, which should become successively smaller as you get to the middle of each arch. Obviously, there isn't anything to split out of or into as you get towards the centre, so notice how I have stitched slightly over the drawn outline of his head, meaning that I will be able to cover the ends of stitches when later working the stitched outline of his face.

18 Next, his face is first outlined in black and then the eyes are filled with stitching as described earlier (*see* Step 3 of the section 'Three-quarter face' in Chapter 3). I have given him blue eyes to match his robe, but you can give him any eye colour that takes your fancy.

His hair is worked with beeswax/warm yellow and fox/ginger brown. Each strand of hair is two rows of colour, layered up to form curls. I have worked outwards from the centre of his forehead, working a layer of the darkest colour first, then snuggling the yellow right up against that. It is normal to have two needles in play for the hair, so that you can fill in each curl strand by strand, as shown in the previous project.

19 He doesn't have a lot of hair, but you don't necessarily have to follow the drawn pattern 100 per cent, as long as it looks about right. You really can't overemphasize the curls of medieval hair, but it is all too easy to flatten them out.

Where the hair meets the halo, remember to slightly overlap it, to cover the ends of the earlier rows of stitching.

His mouth is a simple little stripe of the same fox/ginger brown as used for his hair that you can add whenever you have an appropriate end of silk to use up.

20 Once his hair is styled, it is time to go down to working with two strands of eggshell/pale brown and get on with his skin. Even though I have been doing this form of embroidery for years, I will always begin with the least visible area, especially when switching to a different weight of thread. The face is the focus of the whole image, so, if you are going to make a mistake, or just be a bit rough around the edges until you get your eye in properly, it is best to do that elsewhere – away from the face.

So, it is always feet first, when you have feet present to stitch. For his foot on the right-hand side, it is really just a case of filling from the top, under the hem of the robe, to the tip of each toe, while the left-hand-side foot can be filled as a spiral, to suggest the ball of the foot.

21 Do the hands next: often these are almost as simplistic as are the feet, but, in this case, they are gesturing, so the curled fingers present more of a challenge. Just be sure to fill to the very tip of each digit, splitting out of and into the existing outline.

22 Begin the face in the standard fashion by working the apple of the cheek. In this case, he has rather childlike, chubby cheeks, so, although the apple needs to be high up, it should be big enough to fill most of the side of the face.

23 His head is turned quite far to the side, so, rather than making the far cheek circular, it is best to fill it as a semicircle, working out from the outline, curving across to meet the nose and then curving back under the eye to split into the outline.

24 Sometimes it can be hard to decide where to take the brow line. When this happens, I prefer not to overthink things (that is how projects end up abandoned in the bottom of your workbox for years on end!), because often the cure for indecision is to just get on with it and see what happens – you never learn anything if you don't make mistakes. In this case, I just took the needle and doodled a line across where the contours of his face took me. I began beside the top corner of his ear and went around the outer ear, under one brow, around the nose and over the other brow, before coming back to the starting point at the top of the ear by taking the thread across the back of the work to repeat this stitching sequence. This works for this context because it adds to St Lawrence's slightly quizzical expression.

25 Fill in his brow next by working across the forehead space. I have worked the stitching in one direction, looping across the back of the work to come back to the starting point of this stitching, but you could go back and forth, to add a little frown. Work up from the brows towards the hairline for a more natural look. If you instead follow the hairline and work the flesh of the forehead downwards towards the brow line, you could end up with some very odd lumps to fill in around his brows – he is St Lawrence, not the elephant man. Remember to split out of, and into, the dark outline on each side of his upper face.

26 Once the forehead is filled, you might as well continue working upwards and fill his bald pate, but in this case work down from the top of his head towards the tops of his curls of hair, making sure that the first row of stitching goes over the ends of the rows of stitching already worked for the halo, working ever shortening rows of stitching until the shortest rows are worked into his hair.

If you instead start at his hairline and work outwards, there is a good chance that you will end up with the top of his head being uneven. That top line of his bald head defines the whole shape of the head, so, whereas with hair you can work outwards from the bottom layer and keep adding curls and bouncy bouffant bits until the head looks right, with a bald head, you need to define the outermost edge first.

Plus, those nice long lines of stitching across the top of his head will add shine, and we all know how much men like their bald spots to catch the light, don't we?

27 Fill the nose by following the L-shaped outline of its profile, by working along the two sides until the tip of his nose is filled in. His nose tip is quite square, but, if you fill it as a square by going around all four sides, it won't look like a nose in the end, so just follow the outline until the tip is filled and then work parallel lines of stitching to fill in the rest of the upper shaft of the nose.

28 Next, define the nasolabial lines and then curl the stitching around his chin. It is quite a fiddly small area, so keep your stitches small and always remember to split out of, and into, something.

29 Once the lower part of the chin is filled, work the stitching for the top lip. Note that, once I have filled the upper lip by working a series of lines, I have added a single stitch over the top of this stitching to indicate the philtrum – that little vertical line above the centre lip. Sometimes this addition works and sometimes it doesn't, it is really a judgement call.

30 Connect the apple of the cheek with the chin by working a series of lines of stitching following the shape of the jaw, splitting out of the cheek and into the chin.

31 Fill the underbrow areas next, working the stitching in the direction of his gaze. It is a subtle effect, but it does help to emphasize the eyes if the fill above them is worked to point towards what he is looking at.

32 Start filling the neck in a gentle U-shape to depict the tendons of the neck. This effect can clearly be seen in original works on some larger figures of Christ, where the stitching has worn away to leave a U-shaped line.

33 Finally, fill in all the tiny gaps of flesh remaining between the main areas of stitching. In reality, you may well find it best to fill these small areas as you go along, especially if you have a few inches of thread to use up before threading another needle, but there are always a few such areas that escape and have to be dealt with at the end. Plus, it is always worth peering at the stitching of the face closely for a minute or two, to see whether you missed a bit – and there is no shame in going back and putting an extra stitch in here and there if you see a gap. In all probability, you are likely to be the only person who will ever notice that gap, because we are all our own worst critics, but any gap that you notice is best to deal with now rather than let it bug you forever more.

34 Once that finishing stitching for the face is all done, St Lawrence is all finished and ready to mount as a slip (for more information about working with slips, *see* Chapter 15).

35 Here is the finished slip, mounted on red silk velvet.

CHAPTER 6

UNDERSIDE COUCHING

Underside couching is one of the defining characteristics of opus anglicanum, as one of the two main stitches that are used to work opus pieces. It is a stitch that many students seem to struggle with, but it is quite simple to work once you get the basics right.

Unlike surface couching, where the gold is merely sewn on to the canvas, for basic-stitch underside couching, the gold thread goes through the canvas, but you don't actually sew with it, you just pull a small loop of it through to the back.

So, you are going to be managing two threads at once but only one needle.

This stitch is very hard on the hands: it will roughen your skin and make your fingers ache. So, take care of yourself: limit stitching to no more than forty-five minutes to an hour at each sitting. Even when preparing this book, I limited myself to three sessions of underside couching a day, to avoid hurting my hands.

I have long thought that underside couching was probably a separate job to that of split stitch in a medieval work-shop, purely on the basis that the soft hands needed to handle silk filament are immediately roughened by doing underside couching.

The thread used isn't solid gold but rather gold wrapped around a flexible core. The earliest European gold threads were thinly beaten 24-carat (that is, pure) gold wrapped around a single horsehair, but these had died out by the time that opus anglicanum became popular. Medieval threads, like modern ones, had the metal wrapped around a thread; theirs were normally of silk, modern ones are normally of cotton.

Modern thread is also much cheaper, because it is not made from 24-carat gold any more, or even gilded silver – sometimes it is 2 per cent gold, but often it is just gold-coloured. You can get different shades of gold, as well as silver, and the lovely people at Benton & Johnson even make coloured threads, which aren't authentic but are a lot of fun. All of the passing threads used for the projects throughout this book can be sourced from my website (*see* Suppliers).

Materials

- Ramie or linen fabric canvas
- Passing threads: gold, other-metal (or metal-effect) or coloured
- Large-eyed chenille needle (for example, size 18)
- Strong linen thread, for couching
- Lacing thread
- Beeswax

Shown here are silver, white gold, dark gold and very dark gold, from left to right.

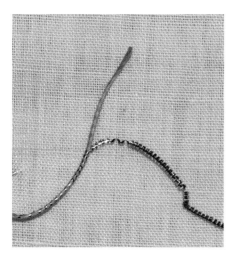

Here you can see an example of both the central thread core and the metal wrapping. The way that the thread is made does make it more delicate than a standard thread of silk or cotton, because, if you treat it roughly, the metal will shred and unwind. The threads that I have used for the examples and projects throughout this book are mostly those known as 'passing', which indicates that you can pass them through the canvas with care, but, if you are ever lucky enough to find vintage threads like the one that I have used for the Rapunzel and Rumpelstiltskin projects, you will find them much more fragile.

Linen thread

For working underside couching, you will also need a strong linen thread. The characteristics of linen threads can vary, and some are stronger than others: Gütermann linen threads need to be doubled, and Duck-brand thread is fabulous if you can find it, but I tend to use a raw linen.

The colour of the linen thread doesn't matter, as you will never see it on the surface of the finished piece: it all goes to the back. The thread should be of around the same thickness as is the gold thread – too thin and it will be more prone to breaking, too thick and it will impede stitching.

Needle threading

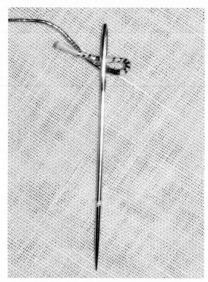

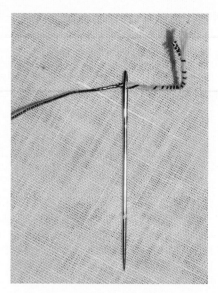

With the fragility of the gold thread in mind, when you do need to use a metal thread with a needle, you don't thread the needle in the usual way, as you would for primarily fibre-based threads. I tend to plunge gold threads with a needle, a needle is used for one project featuring metal thread for some trellis couching, and you will need to use a needle for the making of tassels, if you choose to include them (covered in depth in Chapter 16).

For working with gold or other metal threads, use a large-eyed chenille needle, as shown; I find a size 18 is ideal: the eye is big enough and the needle itself is chunky enough to make a hole in the canvas that the gold can pass through without undergoing much damage.

Don't try to thread the gold by pushing the raw end through the eye, as this will push the gold wrapping off of the thread core. Instead, fold over the very end of the gold thread and push the tip of the resulting loop of gold thread through the eye of the needle.

Once the gold-thread loop tip is sitting within the eye of the needle, gently pull only the loop of gold thread through the eye, no more. The last centimetre or so of metal wrapping may loosen from the thread core, but you are not going to use that bit of the gold thread anyway.

This bit is important: *never* pull the gold thread any further through the eye of the needle – only the folded-over gold thread that formed the threading loop should pass through the eye. If you do pull more of the gold thread through, you will damage the part of the thread that you want to use. That short section of gold thread that passed through the eye isn't going to slip out easily, so, as long as you are careful, it will stay threaded in the needle eye for as long as you need it to. For something like the tassels, where you are going to need the thread in there for a while, you may find that the end starts to shred. In this case, you will have to cut that last centimetre or so off and start again by threading the needle with a fresh end of the gold thread, but, if you are just plunging, there is no need to trim the thread end.

STEP-BY-STEP INSTRUCTIONS

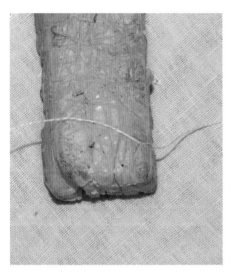

Wax your linen thread (some linen threads are sold already waxed, but these tend to be too thick for our purposes). Pull your working length of linen thread two or three times over a block of beeswax.

You don't need fancy, expensive beeswax; the lumps sold in old-fashioned hardware shops are perfect (and cheap). I tend to bulk buy my beeswax once a year when at my local agricultural show, but a candle will do in a pinch!

Thread your linen on a large chenille needle: again, size 18 is ideal. Selecting a large needle size is important: the thread may seem too dainty for the needle, but there is method in the madness.

You can even find beeswax in the shape of cute little dinosaurs and gold stars. I buy these small blocks to give to students.

Tension

Before we begin to sew, a word about tension. Drum-tight tension gives the best results for your split stitching, but it is even more important when it comes to underside couching.

When I say drum-tight, I mean rock solid, almost incapable of movement. The accompanying photo shows a full bottle of wine, which weighs 1.2kg or 2¾lb, and, as you can see, it is standing on my tightened canvas as comfortably as it would on a table. See how the canvas doesn't dip beneath the weight? That is how tight the canvas needs to be for good underside couching to be achieved.

With decent-quality cloth and use of proper tension, there won't be any significant puckering at the edges of your fabric when you remove it from your frame. The stitches should be packed so closely together that the released canvas shouldn't be bendy enough to pucker, and, even if your canvas does end up wobbling a bit around the edge, to mount opus properly, you are either going to cut that bit off or cover it up, so it doesn't matter.

Also, you might notice in the wine-bottle photo that I tend to do stitch doodles around the edges of my canvas while I work; I know that I will be throwing the edges away, so any mess that I make there doesn't affect the finished piece.

A reminder before you start

As discussed earlier for surface couching, the standard modern practice of plunging the gold thread of each row as a unique end isn't used for underside couching. If you look at the reverse of original pieces of opus anglicanum, the ends are plunged only at the start and at the end of the work, not at the end of each row. This is because:

- It wastes too much thread at the back of the piece, where it won't show and be appreciated. Remember that the medieval threads were of 24-carat gold, or at the very least real silver gilt. The wealthy patrons of opus anglicanum would want every scrap of precious metal accounted for, and they would want it to be on display, not hidden.
- You don't get the right tension on the outer stitches.
- Underside couching allows the surface thread to closely double back on itself, or to return itself: when you pull the final stitch of the row down, you can then easily change the direction of the gold thread.

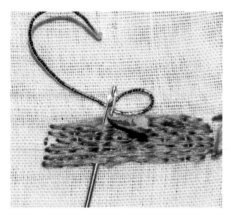

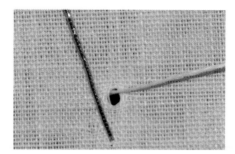

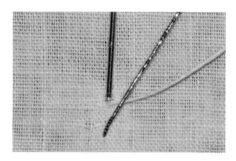

To start off with enough tension on the gold thread, you need to anchor it, which I prefer to do with the help of a large chenille needle. Thread the gold thread as illustrated earlier, with only a centimetre or so of thread extending through the eye of the needle, and take the threaded needle from the front to the back of the work. Don't pull the gold thread all the way through – all you need is enough thread at the back to be able to anchor it, which I like to do by catching it under some nearby stitching worked with silk thread.

Now that you have the gold thread anchored, you can start couching. Anchor your waxed linen thread at the back of the work and bring it up through the canvas at the point where you want to sew, but don't pull it all the way through – leave the needle halfway through the canvas.

One of the biggest problems many people have with underside couching is finding the same hole to go back down again, and the trick is to make it easier to find.

That nice big chenille needle that I told you to use for your linen thread makes a nice big hole, which is easier to find.

But we are going to make it easier still by giving the needle a good wiggle while it is halfway through the canvas, because, if you have the canvas held tight enough, that will make the hole bigger without breaking any of the threads. Aim for a hole of about 1mm in diameter.

Loop the linen thread over the gold thread before popping the needle threaded with the linen thread back down through your easy-to-find hole.

If by some chance you lose track of the hole, or you forgot to wiggle the needle, pull the linen thread firmly to one side and it should open up that hole enough for you to find it again. This is another one of those things that won't work properly if your canvas is too slack.

Now and then you will forget to loop the linen thread around the gold thread, and you will therefore pull the linen thread through the canvas with nothing attached. You are allowed to swear quietly under your breath when this happens.

Once you have the end of the gold thread anchored, you won't need to plunge the gold thread again until you get to the end of the section that you are filling. Sometimes this means having a very long piece of gold thread indeed, so it is better to leave the thread on the reel and unwind it as required.

There is a kind of square-sided wooden reel from Japan called a koma, which won't roll around and is handy if you work with your frame flat. I like to work with my frame at a 45-degree angle, though, and even a square bobbin would roll off, so my preferred method is to keep the reel in a medieval-style drawstring purse tied to the side of the frame. I can pull out as much thread as I need without it going anywhere, and it also deprives the cats of a small thing to steal and destroy, because they aren't good at opening drawstrings.

Tips

If the canvas is too slack, wiggling the needle will just move the canvas around without making the hole any bigger.

Breaking threads in the background canvas will make it lose its structural integrity, which we don't want. This is a big part of the reason for using the finest canvas that you can find. If you use a chunky canvas, you are more likely to pierce it when trying to get the stitch in exactly the right place, whereas, with a fine canvas and a big needle, the threads of the canvas move out of the way of the needle.

Don't worry about the size of the hole; if it doesn't heal up naturally over the next few minutes of your stitching session then the next row of stitching will push it closed.

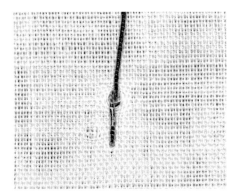

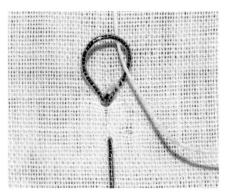

Use the linen thread to pull just a small loop of the gold thread through to the back of the canvas. You have to give it a distinct and firm pull – the gold isn't all that bendy, and, even with that enlarged opening, you have to apply a very small amount of pressure.

Do not yank on the needle. Stressing the whole length of the linen thread will result in frequent breakage. Pull the linen thread through without any force, then grip the couple of centimetres or so of thread left close to the back of the canvas and exert the required amount of pull on this part of the thread and this part alone. By doing this, you stress only the working part of the thread and reduce breakage: the area of stress on the thread moves along the thread as you continue to sew, and the thread is less likely to give up completely and break.

The thread will still break from time to time – all threads break. The aim is to minimize rather than eliminate this event, and remember that this technique is very hard on the linen couching thread.

Tips

Take care not to split the linen couching thread through itself, though, as this will prevent it from fully pulling the gold thread below the canvas (as covered in the next step). If you do happen to inadvertently catch the linen thread in this way, no amount of pulling will work, and your only option is to unpick the linen thread and work the couching stitch again.

Also take care not to break any of the threads of the canvas. This can happen if you miss the hole and pull too hard, but it will weaken the structural integrity of the canvas.

Don't pull the gold thread a long way through the canvas. The aim is to make a kink in the gold thread and pull just that kink or loop through to the back, so that only a little gold dot shows, as illustrated. The hole in the canvas will heal up around the kink (especially when later it is no longer under tension) and therefore hold it firmly in place. It helps to hold the loose end of the gold thread on the front of the work under light tension.

Aim for a little kink, not a big loop, on the back of the work. What you see here is some really terrible underside couching: don't do this.

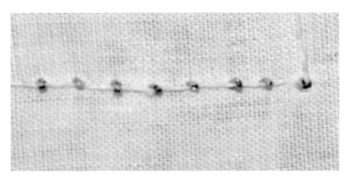

When making each stitch, give a small tug on the gold thread at the front of the work to make sure that there is some tension on it, then feel the stitching on the back. The gold thread at each stitching point should feel like nothing more than a small, rough point.

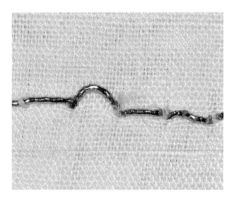

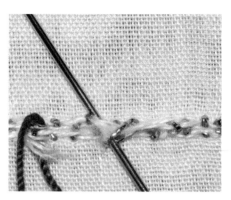

If you do happen to leave big loops of gold thread on the back of the work, they can later push back through the canvas of their own accord and make loops at the front, as shown; this might happen while you are still working on the piece, in which case you will be able to repair it, or it could happen a year later, when there is nothing that you can do about it.

With practice, this unwanted appearance of loops will happen less and less, but, even with experience, you can still miss the odd loop, so it is good practice to always check the back of the work for such loops when you have finished stitching, so that you can fix any that you do find before they pop out. I checked the back of The Three Kings project (see Chapter 11) once I was finished, and I found that I still had one loop to fix.

Again, always check the back of the work for loops before declaring the piece finished. If you find the odd loop, you can indeed fix it.

Once you have done your underside couching properly, the back of the work will be quite raised and a bit rough to the touch, but that means that you can easily sew into the stitching there without affecting the other side of the work. When you find an unwanted loop, just pull it aside and stitch it down into the lengths of linen threads present on the back.

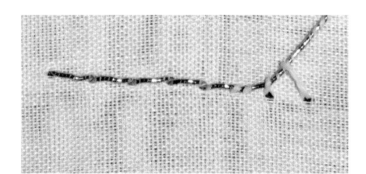

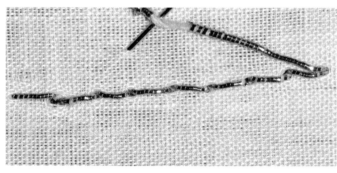

If a loop does pop out on the front of the work, as shown earlier, don't try to fix it by pulling on the gold thread from the front. The gold thread is too rough to flow along the line of stitching, and all that will happen is that you will pull the stitches out completely, as illustrated, and have to start again. Instead, find one end of this loop on the back of the work, and pull on it by hooking a pin or a stiletto underneath it. This is easier said than done, so just do your best to avoid creating a loop in the first place.

Your initial row of underside couching will often look a bit wobbly. This doesn't mean that you are doing something wrong, it is just that the gold kinks where the couching thread touches it. You are going to pack the rows of gold thread so closely and tightly together that the pressure exerted by the subsequent rows will straighten out all the wobbly bits, so they are only temporary. Although lines of underside couching are sometimes used in drapery, they are always made up of several rows of stitching packed together. I am not aware of any piece of original opus anglicanum that uses a solitary row of underside couching for any purpose.

Working efficiently

You can also see here how the couching point creates a natural return or pivoting point for the stitching to change direction. In The Three Kings project in Chapter 11, I will cover how choosing your starting point well can minimize the number of times that you have to start a new piece of thread, but, if you think about it like colouring in, it helps – you are going to go backwards and forwards, not around corners, when you are filling in a large area.

Stitch sizes

As you can clearly see in the accompanying photo, size matters.

Sometimes you will need a stitch as tiny as shown for the top row of stitching, but don't make this your standard size. Use a stitch this small when you are following a pattern, such as the basket-weave pattern as used for The Three Kings project in Chapter 11, or when using one stitch would be too long, but it should be the exception rather than the rule. Not only would it take you forever and a day to fill in your background with stitches of this size but also getting the gold to couch at this stitch length is very difficult – you need a bit of play on the gold thread to couch properly. It also becomes difficult to pack the rows.

The just-right stitches for this technique are somewhere between four and five millimetres in length and never more than six. Stitches of this size couch comfortably, cover the canvas without leaving gaps and are easy to pack.

Remember that too-big stitches will always be too big: gold thread doesn't spread, so, no matter how well you pack stitches of this size, there will be too much movement in the gold thread, and little flashes of white will appear the moment that the canvas moves. The gold thread of these stitches will also bend upwards and get snagged when the canvas moves.

Problems with stitches this long are one of the reasons that patterns worked in underside couching don't get much more complicated than the basket weave that I will use for The Three Kings project. Nearly all of the really complicated patterns belong to the later era of opus, where they are instead executed with surface couching.

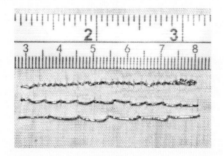

Top: These stitches, barely a millimetre long, are far too small. Middle: This is the baby-bear's porridge of stitches – just right. Bottom: These stitches are too long – way too long.

If you don't pack the gold-thread stitches closely enough together, not only will you see the canvas below but the stitches will stay wobbly, even with the addition of the next rows of stitching. This sample looks a complete mess, doesn't it – but that is to be expected, because the rows of gold are spaced one or two rows of the background canvas apart from one another. Spacing really is important.

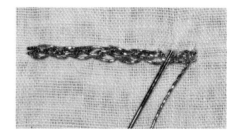

The brick arrangement – where stitches are placed in a brick pattern, with alternate rows being couched in the same place along each row and adjacent rows being couched in an offset position, as for the joints of a brick wall – is by far the most commonly used for underside couching, and it is the one that you should master before trying anything more fancy. In this arrangement, the stitches are also the easiest to pack closely enough together, as shown in this example.

Notice how the couching needle is coming up halfway along the adjacent stitch of the previous row, and almost underneath it – you need to push the previous row of stitching to one side as you go, almost to the point of working slightly underneath it. The gold thread can't spread out in the same way as a fibre-based thread can, so it is really unforgiving of any gaps: it is up to you to make sure that the gaps don't appear.

Tips

Positioning and packing the stitching is something that is easier to do on a properly tight canvas. In fact, if the canvas is tight, you can even reposition a previously made stitch to a certain extent, pushing it back into alignment.

Take care, though, not to damage the metal part of the gold thread with the sharp tip of the needle as you bring up the couching thread. If you break the metal that is wrapped around the cotton core, it will begin to unravel, as illustrated in an image at the start of this chapter, and, if this happens, there is no way of fixing it, other than pulling out the whole row.

Thread breakages

It is inevitable that, from time to time, the linen couching thread will break, no matter how much care you take or how well you wax it before use, because this thread takes a lot of punishment. (Note, however, that I have never broken a gold thread; you shouldn't ever be pulling on it enough to break it.)

I would say that, 99-per-cent of the time, the linen will at least be obliging enough to break at the back of the work, and it is a pretty easy fix. If you have been pulling on the linen thread correctly, and only stressing the two centimetres or so of thread nearest to the canvas, the broken end will usually be quite short, so don't touch it: just leave it alone. This problem needs to be fixed as shown in the accompanying photo.

Once you have made this repair, you can continue working the underside couching as before with the new thread.

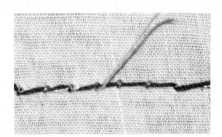

Take a new thread of the same type and colour – I have used a coloured silk thread here so that you can see the repair – and anchor it through the back of the couching before carefully sliding it under the last three or four couching points of the gold thread, starting with the one furthest from the break. This can be a tricky operation when the stitches are massed together, so it helps if you press with a finger from the other side of the canvas to raise the couching points that you are trying to pass the threaded needle under.

Most of the time, you will be placing the edge of your underside couching right alongside silk-filament split stitch; in this case, it is important to make sure that no canvas is visible between the two areas of stitching.

When you are working parallel to the silk stitching, you can push it aside and work slightly underneath it, just as you would when working the underside couching next to more rows of the couching. The silk is a more forgiving neighbour than is the gold thread, though, and will spread a little to cover the interface between the adjacent areas of stitching.

When working at right angles to the silk stitching, be even more careful, as the gold thread will contract a little as you reverse it in order to work the next parallel row of couching, so make sure that you push the gold thread right underneath the adjacent silk stitching.

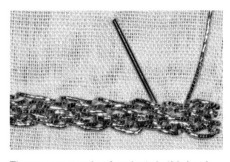

There are a couple of projects in this book – St Michael and the Dragon (see Chapter 7) and Selfie Girl (see Chapter 14) – that feature a diagonally couched, or twill, pattern, and you will notice that I never mark the diagonal on the canvas: I just work this twill couching by eye, as has been done for the example shown here. By all means, try marking the diagonal on a sample canvas and see how you go, but nearly everyone finds it easier to do it by eye.

It is actually quite difficult to mark the diagonal on the correct angle, so, nine times out of ten, you end up wandering away from it as you stitch, and the marks on the canvas then become confusing.

Tips

The diagonal is easier to stitch by eye because all you have to do is follow on from each previous row of couching by offsetting each stitch by about one millimetre instead of putting it dead centre as you would with the brick-pattern arrangement of stitches, and the diagonal couching will grow organically from there.

Try both ways, with a marked diagonal line and without, but do this on a sample canvas, and then use whichever approach works best for you when making your embroidery.

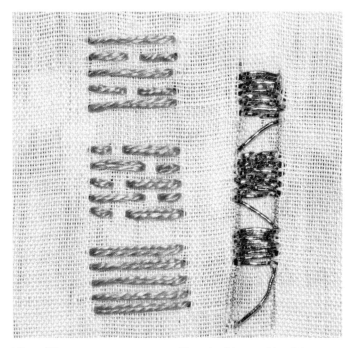

When filling a very narrow space with underside couching, it is tempting to save time and effort by simply working back and forth, as shown at the bottom of the two columns of stitching, almost as if you were working satin stitch. There are two reasons not to do this:

- The resulting stitch texture will be different. When you are filling in the background of a piece with underside couching, the aim is to create a homogeneous mass of gold, and changing the texture of one small area, by working the stitching in a different manner, will draw the eye to it in an undesirable way.
- You can see, even in my small sample, that the stitches don't lie as flat when they are all couched at the same point. Again, this changes the appearance of this area of stitching in a distracting and undesirable way, and these stitches could be more prone to being caught or snagged.

Even for long stretches of narrow underside couching, it is best to use a brick arrangement.

The middle block of stitching is the best option when the area to be covered is more than one stitch wide but not quite two: this is basically a staggered brick-and-a-half arrangement.

The top block of stitching shows the pattern to use when your gap is roughly one stitch wide, so you span the entire gap with one stitch, then couch the adjacent stitch in the middle, that is, halfway along it – exactly as if you were laying a narrow course of actual bricks.

CHAPTER 7

St Michael and the Dragon, from the Syon Cope

TECHNIQUES

Dragon, drapery, feathered wings, halo, herringbone-twill couching, segmented wings, silk underside couching, surface couching of details, underside couching for filling of objects (rather than background)

This design, taken from the Syon Cope, relies far less on the layering of colours and drapery to create an image than the other pieces of opus anglicanum that we are looking at. Instead, the colours are treated as solid blocks and interest is added by using underside couching. Unusually, the underside-couching technique is used here for both the drapery and the angel's wings, and also for the background, where a chunky silk is couched to fill the area instead of the usual gold thread. It might seem like a lot of underside couching, and it is, but, because there are no complicated patterns embedded within the areas of couching, you can concentrate on basic technique instead; by the time you finish this piece, you will have gained confidence to tackle more complex patterns worked

with underside couching, which we will examine in subsequent projects.

The subject is the Archangel Michael slaying the devil in the form of a dragon, and there are numerous versions of the image found throughout medieval art. Before about AD1500, all medieval dragons are classed as wyverns by modern taxon-

omy, because they only ever have two legs rather than four, but, by medieval terms, they are dragons. I love the fact that this one has a cheeky second head on the end of his tail, which looks as if it is about to reach up and nip St Michael's elbow. I also love the passivity of the angel's gaze, which is typical of medieval saints, because

he looks like he is just so bored with all of this dragon slaying when he would much rather watch Netflix and just chill.

There are also some wonderful depictions of St Margaret of Antioch and the dragon in medieval embroidery. She was supposedly swallowed by Satan, again in the form of a dragon, but she made the sign of the cross and her crucifix grew so huge that she burst out of the beast's belly. Obviously, this is a tricky subject to draw, so medieval artists sort of spliced Margaret into the dragon's back, so that she looks more like she is riding a particularly ugly pony. Here, St Michael appears to be surfing casually upon the back of the beast that he is about to slay.

Materials

Fabric
- Double layer of fine ramie or linen fabric (60 to 80 count), 50cm × 50cm (about 20in × 20in)

Needles
- Size 8 crewel needle
- Size 18 chenille needle

Threads
- Silk-filament DeVere Yarns 6 thread, one 200m reel each in the following shades:
  - 01 white
  - 09 salmon/apricot
  - 45 green
  - 55 beeswax/warm yellow
  - 56 lotus/very dark blue
  - 57 star/mid blue
  - 112 dutch/dusty blue
  - 129 liquorice/dark grey
  - 137 cigar/very dark brown
  - 261 ginger/russet
  - 1061 pearl/flesh
    Please note that one whole reel of each colour is more than adequate for the working of this project: any thread remaining can be used for the working of several other projects.
- Silk-filament DeVere Yarns 60 thread, one 25m reel each in the following shades:
  - 44 black ebony
  - i90 ingot/gold
- 2/5nm spun-silk thread, madder-dyed, 30g (alternatively, use a different thick spun silk)
- Benton & Johnson smooth passing no 6, one 50m spool each in the following shades:
  - black
  - dark gold
  - silver
- Benton & Johnson smooth passing no 5, one 50m spool in very dark gold
  Please note that one whole spool each of smooth passing is more than adequate for the working of this project: any passing thread remaining can be used for the working of several other projects.
- Strong linen thread, for couching
- Lacing thread

Additional materials
- Beeswax, for waxing linen thread

1 Transfer the pattern on to the cloth. The barbed quatrefoil is a much more geometric shape than an initial glance would suggest (and a lot of common medieval decorative elements are), but don't fret too much if your lines go a big wonky.

Tip

Normally, I don't advocate stitching the entire outline with one colour, as this can look heavy, but there are exceptions, and the outlines for this project are one such instance.

2 Outline the design with four strands of cigar/very dark brown. Don't outline the outside of the quatrefoil border, the dragon's claws and the dragon's inner stripes: those are better defined later.

All of the stitched filling is to be worked with four strands of thread, unless otherwise stated.

In places – the bottom curves of the angel's wing feathers, the inner folds of the gown and the outer edge of the dragon's

wing – add a bit more depth by working a double row, the second being split out from the first.

However, you may want to outline the upper-wing feathers now with lotus/very dark blue; I chose to change the original outlining at a later stage – *see* steps 26–27, where discussing how to replicate the tarnishing of silver in present-day embroideries.

3 Use a little bit of green silk to fill the shaft of Michael's spear. One needleful of silk should be just enough to do one pass, so go back to the starting point with a new thread, rather than working back and forth.

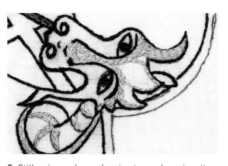

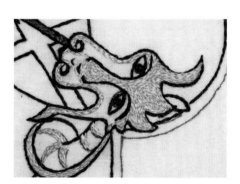

4 Salmon/apricot is used for working one row of feathers, just above the flight feathers, and for the spine and details of the dragon – the tongue and eyebrow of the secondary head, the eyebrow ridge of the primary head and the spine, as well as the stripes that define the shape of the dragon's wing.

The dragon's little stripes need to be both tapered into triangles and slightly curved to emphasize the shape of his body. This is done with the same technique as creating points in drapery. He is very much a wyrm-like dragon: long and sinuous.

5 Still using salmon/apricot, work a circuit of stitching down from his lower horn (or it could be an ear) to his nose and back up again to the upper horn/ear. After a couple of passes, the bridge of his nose will be solidly filled, so continue a smaller circuit around the end of his nose until that is filled too.

Next, follow the circuit up from his nose to outline his quiff.

6 Circle around and fill in the shape formed by his quiff at the centre of his head before splitting out rows of stitching into his horns/ears. Remember to always split something, so that each row of thread building up the horns/ears is split out from the stitching of the quiff and is then split down, either into another salmon/apricot stitch or into the bordering outline.

Define the lower half of his face by working a row starting from his beard, moving around the edge of his mouth and under one nostril, skipping under his nose between his nostrils and working up the other side of his face. Repeat working along this stitching route until the narrower areas are filled, and then define the shape below his nose.

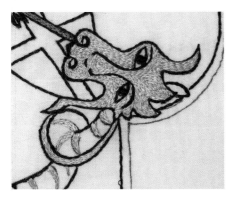

7 Fill the remaining areas of his face by following the direction of the existing stitches. Remember to always split out of or into another stitch.

8 Use a few white stitches to fill the eyes. You can do this stitching for the eyes of both heads of the dragon and of the angel at the same time.

Also, add a single row of white stitching around the outside of the inner quatrefoil border.

Highlight the edges of the hanging part of the angel's robe.

9 Dutch/dusty blue is used for stitching the dragon's wing. Work all of the stitches down and out from the top of the wing (under the angel's feet), maintaining a unified direction by skipping over the back of the work to get back to the top of the next segment. There is also a tiny spot of dutch/dusty blue filling added for each of the dragon's nostrils.

Add some shape to his body with stripes consisting of tiny triangles of dutch/dusty blue between the salmon/apricot stripes for four segments on each side of the wings.

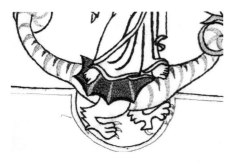

10 The triangular stripes need to be only a few stitches long and don't need to go all the way across the body, as shown here. As for the salmon/apricot stripes, these stripes need to be tapered and slightly curved, to emphasize the form of the dragon's body.

11› Star/mid blue is used for both the rest of the dragon's body and the border.

For the circuits of stitching for the border, I did five rows, but more is fine. Make sure that you keep the corners nice and square; working into a corner, be sure to split right into the previous row to avoid letting the row curve, and, when working out, end the line with a half stitch, then split out of that so that the corner stays sharp. (The section on Mitred Corners in Chapter 12 gives further advice.)

Work the dragon's body segments from top to bottom, just as you did for the wings, being sure to split out of and into the border. Keep the direction of stitching unified, and practice layering where the segments splay out.

Stitch down one side of the dragon's leg, into the first toe, and then skip under the foot to the toe on the opposite side to start stitching upwards again. As with his nose, continue on this stitching path until the narrower segments of the foot are completely filled, then fill any remaining areas by working in a spiral. Work the second foot in the same manner.

Tip

Working the stitching for the border is a nice task for when you want a brainless job to do, because you just need to work around in a continuous circuit until the stitching is as thick as you want it to be.

12 Add some beeswax/warm yellow to his collar and the very bottom of his robe, using four strands still. Also, fill in the triangular areas of drapery with liquorice/dark grey. I tend to avoid using stark blacks and favour greys and dark browns for this, because I find that black can be too dominant, as it just doesn't play well with the other colours, but, in this case, I also wanted to reserve the use of actual black as a heraldic colour for the shield. The contrast here is subtle but important.

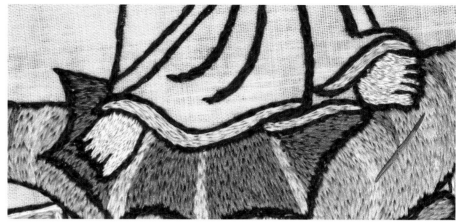

13 For the flesh, go down to working with two strands of pearl/flesh. On the principle of starting with the area that draws the least attention, begin with the feet. Even if you have been stitching for days on end, going down to half the thickness of thread can be a shock to the system, so there is no harm in starting with the area where people are least likely to notice any mistakes that you do happen to make.

Work down from the ankle – or rather the part of the foot nearest to the ankle that is visible beneath the robe – and work down into the toes before going back to the beginning of the row by skipping up the back of the work and continuing to stitch all of the remaining rows in the same direction until the foot is coloured in. There will be some partial rows to work where the flesh colour needs to split into the dark outlines.

Remember to always split out of or into the outline around the feet.

Tip

For opus anglicanum, sometimes there really isn't any attempt at showing shape in the draperies – here, they are just solid blocks of colour – so simply remember to always split something, work in a coherent direction and pack the stitches really tightly together, and everything will be fine.

14 The hands are worked upon much the same principle as are the feet, working from the wrists to the fingertips. I have introduced curved stitches on the heel of the hand that holds the shield, but it is not absolutely necessary.

15 Often, I will start working on the face by defining the line of muscles in the neck and connecting them with the apple of the cheek, and, as you can see, I started to do that here before I realized there was a lock of hair in the way. In this case, it is best to start by defining the round part of each cheek. Because the face is seen in three-quarter profile, the right-hand-side cheek as we look at the canvas isn't worked as a circle but by fanning out the curves of the stitching to fill the space.

16 Begin the forehead by splitting out of the cheek and working up the side of the face before continuing over the forehead.

Angels, unlike opus prophets who often have saggy faces, are far too serene to have crow's feet, so try to pack your stitches together until our angel's face is as smooth as a baby's bottom.

Work the forehead in rows, each splitting out from the first vertical line laid down, and fan these rows out to fill the space, but don't worry about the little bits around his hair right now.

17 Next, work the nose by splitting out from the forehead and following the nose's outline downwards, then come back up to the forehead, split out again, and work down the nose shaft until the nose is filled.

18 Now work the jawline in the same fashion, splitting out from below the ear, working down the jaw and at first going around the nasolabial line to form a muzzle shape. Work a circle within the lower part of the muzzle shape to form the chin. Then work the upper lip as a half circle from one side of the mouth to the other. Fill the jawline with a solid block of stitches all worked in a unified direction. Finally, add some directional filling stitches to connect the chin area to the far cheek.

You will probably also need to use some triangular filling stitches to fill the tiny gaps around the nose.

Tip

Remember to always split something and to work blocks of stitches in a unified direction. Pack the rows of stitches so closely together that sometimes you will think you have just done the same row twice. And, if you look at part of the stitching with which you thought you had covered the canvas and you see the tiniest hint of background fabric, there is no shame in going back and putting some extra stitches in.

Another reminder!

Throughout the opus projects, I will nag you about always splitting something and working blocks of stitches in a unified direction, and about packing these stitches tightly. It is not that I am forgetting what I have already written; it is because this is the single most important thing that you can do to make your stitching look polished with this technique. Splitting these tiny, almost-impossible-to-see stitches when working the face will make the skin look like one membrane, whereas visible ends of rows and individual stitches will stick out like the proverbial sore digit and destroy the harmony of the image. So, I will nag you, and then I will nag you again, because this is the most fundamental thing to do in order to get opus anglicanum right.

19 Fill the areas under the eyebrows by splitting out from the initial forehead line that leads up the side of the face and then splitting into the side of the nose.

Also, work the triangular spaces beneath the eyes by matching the direction of the spiral stitching of the cheek.

20 Fill the neck by working rows of stitching in a U-shape from one side of the neck to the other, to reflect the shape of the sinews. Work the upper half of the neck until it is filled, and then create a contrast by working to fill the rest of the neck area below this stitching in the opposite direction.

21 Last but not least, fill the tiny triangular areas around the hair by working the stitching in the same direction as of the forehead stitches.

The final effect of all this subtle and carefully considered stitch placement is a face that is clearly well modelled and three-dimensional, even though it is completely flat. This modelling relies largely on the reflective sheen of the silk – it is about the material as much as the technique, and, although you can echo it with cotton, it will never be more than a pale imitation.

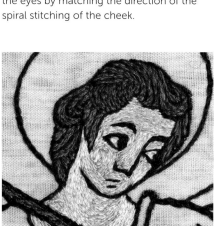

22 Go back up to using four strands of thread, this time for his hair. The previous figures had hair worked in a two–two pattern, that is, using two threads of a lighter colour and also two threads of a darker colour to work alternate rows of stitching, but this angel has one row of cigar/very dark brown for every two rows of ginger/russet, to give a more subtle effect. Have fun putting some swirls and bounce into the hair – opus angels seem to spend a lot of time at the salon getting bouffant hairdos.

23 Now that all of the split-stitch embroidery has been done, it is time to move on to the underside couching, with gold, silver and black passing as the surface threads and linen thread for the couching thread.

Most of this piece is done with very simple couching, but first working around all of the fold lines of the tunic is very good practice. Use very dark gold passing no 5 for the first part. You are basically colouring in the under tunic, keeping all of the couching going on a vertical axis. I find that I prefer

to work underside couching from side to side, building the stitching away from my body, so, because I use a floor-standing frame, I will usually set my frame up with the image on its side with this approach in mind. I am so habituated to working underside couching in this way that, if I forget, I will take the canvas off and reset it before starting to couch, so it is a good idea to work a small test sampler to decide how you like to work before working any underside couching for an actual embroidery.

Tips

Tension is really important for underside couching, so stop now and retension your canvas, because the best results are obtained with a drum-tight canvas. When I say 'drum tight', I don't just mean that it makes a little noise when you tap on it, I mean that a significantly heavy item could stand on top of the canvas and for the fabric to barely dip.

Also, leave the underside couching for the cross on the end of his spear until last, as it is by far the fiddliest bit, so it is best to get your eye in first.

Tip

Pay extra care to tightly pack the stitches when using black. Covering a light colour with a dark, and vice versa, will show every little mistake and gap.

A note about thread choice

The biggest challenge here was finding the right silk for the job of underside couching the background pattern. The one used in the original has a dull appearance and is fairly hefty, giving a beautiful textural contrast to the lustre of the central images.

I ordered samples of all sorts of things before finding exactly the right thing in one of my stash boxes and which was the result of a dye experiment. The chosen 2/5nm thread is a spun silk, not the shining filament silk used elsewhere: it is soft and almost cottony, with a very soft drape. (Como silk was the second best for this job, but I feel it is just a tiny bit too shiny.)

24 Use dark gold passing no 6 for working the palla, or over robe, and the halo in the staggered brick pattern of underside couching. Because both parts of his outfit are worked with the same stitch and in the same direction, the slight difference in colour and weight of the gold threads makes a very subtle contrast.

Pack your couching really closely and tightly, remembering to work slightly under the lines of silk stitching. You can get away with having a few tiny areas of white canvas showing here because they will be covered by the slight shrinking of the canvas when you remove the tight tension, but try to keep these white areas to an absolute minimum, as seen here, where they are highlighted by flash photography.

Don't forget to fill the small triangles of his folded robe where it hangs from his shoulder.

25 The bright silver passing no 6 is used for working the cross on the shield, the spear tip pointing out from the dragon's head, and the flight feathers of St Michael's wings. In this case, it is much easier to work in the direction of the design rather than straight up and down.

26 In the original cope, the whole of each wing was worked in silver, which has tarnished over time. I suspect that, when the cope was in regular use, it would have had the silver areas gently burnished before each wearing to restore the original shine, but this is obviously something that a modern conservator would forbid, for fear of damaging the now-very-delicate threads.

There are long-standing debates in art history over what silver would look like, with many arguing that it would be blackened by tarnish most of the time. I have chosen to play on this idea to create more contrast in the wings by using a modern passing – black passing no 7 – to fill the upper part of the wing, partly because I am interested to see how much the silver tarnishes to match it over time.

27 Once I had put the tarnish-like black passing in place, however, I wasn't happy with how poorly the brown outline of the wings and their feathers showed, so I chose to work over it with lotus/very dark blue. The outline is still subtle, but I like the oily, crow's-wing look of it. It is quite difficult to work split stitch over underside couching, though, so, if you prefer the blue look, I would advise you to learn by my mistake and put the blue in place along with the initial outline.

28 At this point, all of the split stitch and all of the metal-thread underside couching are complete. All that is left to do is the silk-thread underside couching and the dragon's claws.

29 The Syon Cope includes a lot of underside-couched silk. We are not going to use the fine DeVere Yarns 6 threads for this first stage, as the underside-couched silk provides a lovely textural contrast to the rest of the piece; instead, we will use DeVere Yarns 60 threads, which is basically ten strands of the 6 thread lightly twisted together: it has much of the same high shine and lustre as the 6 thread but a lot more body.

The first step is to fill the narrow borders of the robe with ingot/gold. If you have left the gaps between the areas of the previously made stitching nice and evenly spaced, this should be a quick job, as you won't need to work more than two or three rows of stitching. Instead of using the brick-pattern couching employed for the robes and wings, emphasize the borders by placing your linen-thread couching stitches side by side, to make little square blocks of silk, as shown here.

30 Continuing with 60 thread, use black ebony to fill the blank areas of the shield that Michael is so merrily jamming down the poor dragon's throat, but go back to using the same staggered brick pattern that we used for working the robes. Don't worry about making the stitching perfectly vertical; follow the upright lines of the cross and it will be filled in far better. Be careful as you use this silk: it likes to catch on any snag in your nails just as much as the 6 thread does.

31 The penultimate task is to couch the background in a herringbone-twill pattern.

Work so that your rows of couching threads are vertical to the central image, as in the original. This means starting at the apex of one of the small arches and working outwards. I prefer to work underside couching from side to side, so you can see here that I rotated my frame to get a more comfortable working angle. Work at the angle that is most comfortable for you.

Herringbone-twill couching

Couch this thread in exactly the same way as the gold passing threads, but note that, because it is soft, it is much easier to use, and, being considerably thicker, it also makes filling the background a relatively quick job in terms of underside couching.

For the background herringbone-twill couching, if you wish, you can mark out the zigzag on the canvas, but one of the problems is that everyone has an angle that they are happy working at, and it varies from person to person – mark the wrong angle on the canvas and all you have is some confusing scribbles. Unlike the basket-weave pattern used later for The Three Kings design, this doesn't have to be all that precise, and, in practice, I have found that most students prefer working without marking this design, as it is easier to work it as a sort of organic progression.

Work your first row of couching just as you would for the standard staggered brick pattern that we used before, still using the linen thread as the couching thread. However, because the surface thread is thicker than metal passing, make each stitch about 20-per-cent longer, to accommodate for the thread being wider. Then, work your next row by staggering the couching point by a quarter of a stitch length and – *voilà* – you have created a twill pattern!

It really is that simple; you don't need to do any complicated geometry. When you want to reverse the direction, to zig rather than zag, just stagger the stitch in the opposite direction, again by shifting the couching point by a quarter of a stitch length each time. Try to lay down a set number of rows in one direction before reversing and working the same number in the other direction. I aimed for seven each way, but I am a bit rubbish at counting, so some of my reversals are after eight rows. But, if you really squint closely at the original, it is not perfect or geometrically precise either: the original is a bit on the wibbly wobbly side too, which is why I am convinced that the original embroiderers were eyeballing it as well.

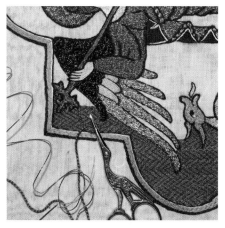

32 Keep filling upwards and outwards, rotating your frame as necessary for stitching comfort, keeping the silk on the surface and following a single line of stitching until a particular area is full before finishing the end of the line and starting to fill in the next area. Avoid the temptation to 'sew' with this silk; don't plunge it more often than you need to because it is not only soft but is really too thick for this canvas, so, if you go in and out with it too much, it will shred just as quickly as the gold passing would.

33 Work around the piece until the whole of the background is filled in. You can see here that any minor irregularities in the herringbone really don't show.

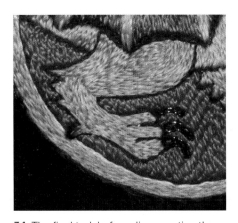

34 The final task before slip mounting the finished embroidery is to give the dragon a manicure, which I have done by surface couching some black passing no 7 into claw shapes. You could use gold or silver passing, but I think dragons probably have dirty fingernails, so I opted for the black.

35 Now, you can slip-mount him (*see* Chapter 15).

CHAPTER 8

THE CHERUB: A SAMPLER OF WINGS

TECHNIQUES

Drapery, feathered underside couching, feathered wings, interlaced wings, peacock eyes, simple halo

Angels with more than one pair of wings are cherubs, and they are often used as filling designs in between the main panels of a cope.

There are so many ways of dealing with wings in opus anglicanum that I couldn't possibly show all of them, but I have picked out a six-winged angel from the Syon Cope as an example with which to show you as many variations as possible. Obviously, you may want to pick one wing design and use it throughout or to even our angel up with three matching pairs of wings, but you can also use this design as a sampler to try as many different designs as possible. If you do decide to go for the mismatched option shown here, it is worth bearing in mind that, on the Syon Cope, some of the cherubs do indeed have mismatched wings, even to the extent of the left and right wings not matching. There is no way of knowing whether this was a result of two

Materials

Fabrics
- Double layer of fine ramie or linen fabric (60 to 80 count), 25cm × 30cm (about 10in × 12in)
- A piece of velvet of about the same size as the double-layer ramie or linen fabric, as the top layer of the silk–ramie (or –linen) canvas

Needles
- Size 8 crewel needle
- Size 18 chenille needle

Threads
- Tram silk thread, one 10g spool each in the following shades:
  - brown
  - dark cream
  - green
  - light blue
  - light cream
  - purple
  - teal
  - turquoise

    Please note that one whole spool of each colour is more than adequate for the working of this project: any thread remaining can be used for the working of several other projects.
- Como silk thread, one 10g spool in shade blanco
- 30/2nm spun-silk thread (DeVere Yarns 36 thread will also work), one 10g spool each in the following shades:
  - ecru
  - sky blue

    Please note that one whole spool of each colour is more than adequate for the working of this project: any thread remaining can be used for the working of several other projects.
- Benton & Johnson smooth passing no 5, one 50m spool, in silver

    Please note that one whole spool is more than adequate for the working of this project: any passing thread remaining can be used for the working of several other projects.
- Strong linen thread, for couching
- Lacing thread

Additional materials
- Beeswax, for waxing linen thread

different people working on the same figure or perhaps of one stitcher covering part of the design and forgetting which style of wing had been done already – who knows?

I am going to work this figure with tram, spun and Como silks, rather than the more expensive silks produced strictly for embroidery. Tram and Como silks are both filament silks, but they are produced for weaving rather than sewing. Tram silk is very similar to DeVere Yarns filament silk, but the tram silk is of a slightly heavier denier, so it is a great silk for learning purposes.

The tram silks that I have used come from The Handweavers Studio & Gallery (and they can be bought from other weaving suppliers too) in 10g spools, which are considerably larger than those supplied for embroidery. However, the tram silk is cheaper and slightly chunkier than the DeVere Yarns threads, so it is a great practice thread and handy to have in your stash. A 10g spool will last for many projects, and you could use the shades of this project for working some of the other projects in this book if you change many of the basic colours used for them, if you don't want to match the colours shown exactly.

Como silk is a twisted filament that you have to unply before use, in much the same way you would for a standard cotton embroidery thread; it has got a bit more body and bounce than the flatter tram silk and looks less shiny, much like the silks used in original pieces, and many beginners find it easier to handle. Como silk also comes in 10g spools, which I again get from The Handweavers Studio & Gallery in the form of a twisted filament. It is great to have around in its twisted form for braided edges, tassels (note that I have used it for the purse assembly covered in Chapter 16) and even underside couching.

It is worth remembering that both of these silks are sold in hefty ten-gram spools, but, metre for metre, they work out significantly cheaper than similar silks sold for embroidery, so they are great for experimenting with or for really large projects.

The disadvantage of both of these silks is their more limited colour ranges, but that can also be an advantage. Throughout this book, I will encourage you to change colours to suit your own tastes, but I will also emphasize the importance of limiting your colour palette for a more authentic feel. When you look at original opus pieces, they do have limited palettes of perhaps only three or four shades of each colour, because that would have been all that was available at the time. Working within a limited palette can be very freeing, because you can use only what you have, instead of fretting about whether you have picked the wrong shade of pink from the two hundred or so that you don't have – again, if you have only three blues, those are the three blues you use!

The last thread type used for this project is 30/2nm spun silk. Once again, this comes in 10g spools that I source from The Handweavers Studio & Gallery. This thread is basically of the same weight as standard sewing cotton, and we will use it in this project for wings, but you could use a tram silk or other filament silk instead, if you prefer.

I have chosen a blue-and-silver palette for my angel because I fancied him in wintry colours, but you could just as easily work him in a palette for any of the other seasons, or even in rainbow colours – pink and purple would look gorgeous too. Using him as a sampler is the perfect opportunity to play with colour.

STEP-BY-STEP INSTRUCTIONS

1 Transfer the design on to your canvas, but don't worry too much about getting every feather precisely right.

2 Use four strands of brown tram silk for working the initial outline. Often, I will vary the colour of the silk that I use for the outlines within one project, to stop it from looking flat overall, but there is going to be a lot going on here with so many different wings, so I am unifying the chaos by using a single outline colour.

As you can see here, I haven't outlined absolutely everything; some of the flight feathers, the wings covering the body, and the little ball that he is standing on have been left alone for now. This is because these feathers are going to be worked in a variation of underside couching that is easier to execute without an outline being present.

3 We will deal with the flesh and drapery first, before moving on to our cherub's assorted feathery bits. Continue by using four strands, now of teal, to add the darkest layer of shading to his drapery. I am saying drapery because I think it is meant to be some sort of angelic tunic, but, let's face it, it looks like a scarf, doesn't it?

Use a spot of this colour to fill in the background quarter circles of the little ball that he is standing on.

4 Use turquoise for the middle layer of shading of his scarf. I am going fairly heavy with this colour and leaving only a sliver of space for the highlight, because I want him to be covered by a lovely celestial blue.

5 Next, fill in the gaps of the scarf with a light-blue highlight.

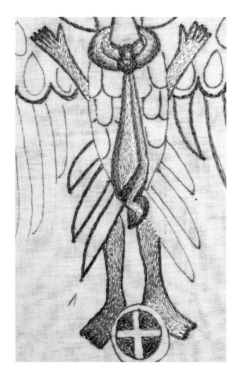

‹**6** I am using dark cream for the flesh, which is a properly pasty opus flesh colour. However, remember to use just two strands for working the flesh.

His hands and feet are filled in a very linear fashion, with almost no attempt at shaping or modelling; as he was originally just a filler pattern, he wasn't treated as carefully as the star turns in the main panels.

And, yes, I know that I have given my version two left feet: I have adjusted the drawing for tracing for you. Angels fly by dancing anyway: his feet are just for decorative purposes.

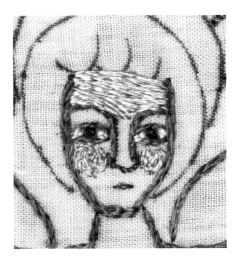

7 His face is very small. I can almost cover it with my thumb, so it is never going to look as polished as do the big faces from the previous chapters, but it is treated in the same way as the frontal face. So, start by working two tiny apples for his cheeks. Next, add some blanco Como silk stitching to his eyes. The Como should be split down into 1/16th of the full strand for a finer thread.

8 Now, work across his forehead, packing the stitches closely and tightly together. Use the brown outline to split out of and into at the beginning and end of each row.

9 Work his nose by splitting out of the forehead so that the stitches blend. His nose isn't big enough to try curving the stitches around the tip, so work each row downwards and split into the outline instead.

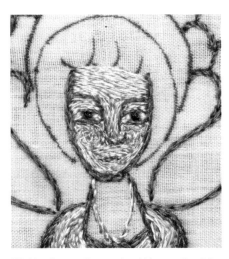

10 His face is too small to try working an apple for his chin, so it is best to concentrate on the jawline instead. Split out of the cheek on one side, work across below the mouth and then split back into the cheek on the other side.

11 Fill his upper lip by working all of the necessary rows in the same direction, from cheek to cheek, then fill the skin below the brows, as well as all of the little corners that remain on the face.

12 I inadvertently smudged his mouth a bit when I was filling his chin, so I have gone over that with a little more brown before working a U-shape to start his neck (this is to represent the same diagonal tendon that you see for the neck of a three-quarter-profile face). Remember that it is always fine to re-emphasize a line if you feel that this is needed.

13 Next, fill his neck, following the direction of the stitches worked in the U-shape and always remembering to split out of and into the previous rows of stitching.

14 His hair is worked as rows of one strand of brown that are layered with rows of two strands of light blue. Hair colours in opus are not always naturalistic, but, in this case, the light blue shades towards silvery grey, for a bit of a science-fiction look.

15 The wings around our angel's head are upside down, so the top of the wing is at the bottom, nearest his head. I started with teal, then went on to green and turquoise, and finally used light blue for the long flight feathers. Work each feather as an individual shape, curling around at the tip. The long flight feathers should be worked along their length, even when they are interlaced with another set of feathers, as they are here. By working the two opposing sets of flight feathers in their natural direction of growth, you will add a subtle textural contrast to the interlacing.

Interlacing always looks intimidating and chaotic, but it actually works on strict rules – one under, one over. As long you remember that rule, it is easy.

Sometimes a very plain wing is jazzed up by having one of the feather layers worked instead with underside couching, as for the flight feathers of St Michael's wings in the Syon Cope project, but bear in mind that that particular project is based on a figure from a main panel.

Wings

The simplest form of wing in opus anglicanum is also the most common. The feathers are outlined and then filled with flat colour, with each tier of feathers being filled with a different shade. Sometimes the colours contrast; sometimes they are all shades of the same colour – usually worked from the darkest shade at the top of the wing through to the lightest for the flight feathers, but not always in this order.

Most of the angels in opus aren't the star turn. Some get the spotlight in the main panels, such as St Michael on the Syon Cope panel, but most of them are just hanging around in the margins, playing music or dancing, so they don't warrant the same showy treatment, and this probably accounts for the popularity of the plain wing.

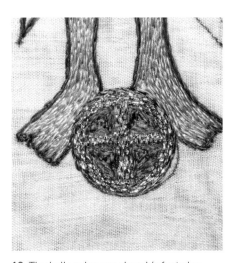

16 Simple wings can also be filled with a spine running down the middle of each feather. Whether you insert the spine before filling or after is up to you: it is perfectly reasonable to work a spine over the top of an existing plain wing if you decide that it needs a bit more detail.

I worked my feather spines first, in green, to balance the row of green feathers on the other wing (although there is no symmetry to the layout of the wings, you can still make the design harmonious by balancing the colours, though this will make no difference to those who get upset by asymmetry). I have stitched simple little green spines of just two rows of split stitch, but often, in original pieces, the spines will have a dark outline as well.

I have worked teal at the base, as for the plainest wing, then missed out the layer of green feathers and gone straight on to using turquoise, light blue and then light cream for the long flight feathers, so that there is contrast within the interlacing.

While working up at the head, work two rows of purple to outline the outer edge of the halo.

17 The halo is really too narrow to do anything fancy with, so just fill it with plain underside couching with silver.

18. The ball under our cherub's feet also needs some underside couching. Fill the inner cross in the usual back-and-forth manner, and, for the outer circle, you could do the same; however, this is the perfect opportunity to try working underside couching in a spiral. Start from the inside of the circle and work outwards to get an even finish. Make the stitches of the first, inner row a bit smaller than usual, because, as you hit each starting point of the next round of the outward spiral, the stitches of each subsequent row will need to get slightly bigger, to conform to the shape of the circle.

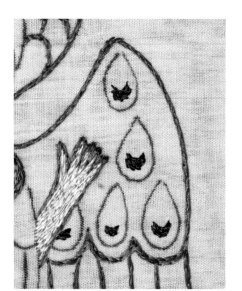

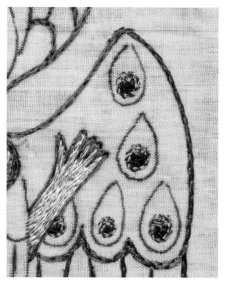

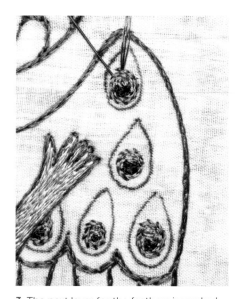

1 Peacock wings are quite common on cherubs, and the easiest place to start the stitching is with the numerous feather eyes. In this instance, I have marked teardrop shapes for the eyes, but you can just mark the central spots, taking care to allow enough space for each one.

Begin with a little crescent or a heart shape – either is fine, as the stitches are quite small, so go with whichever form you find easier to make – of purple. Note that this shape is positioned slightly off-centre for each eye, towards the base of the teardrop.

2 Still using four strands, of green this time, work around each crescent to encircle it. Make the green into a full circle, rounding out the top of each crescent to create the distinctive shape at the centre of a peacock feather. Keep the stitches small, as, unless you supersize the wing, you will need only one complete outer row of green around the purple.

3 The next layer for the feathers is worked with teal. Again, this is mostly just one row around, but, because we are aiming for an egg-shaped oval rather than a circle, it equates to two rows at the top.

Note that, for the second eye from the top, I brought the needle out on the upper right of the previous row of green stitching and worked around anticlockwise (though it doesn't matter whether you go clockwise or anticlockwise when working a circle, you will probably find you do one or the other without thinking about it).

The uppermost eye shows a completed circle worked in the same manner, anticlockwise, but notice that I haven't ended where I began; instead, I have overlapped the first few stitches, to add volume and an oval profile to the shape.

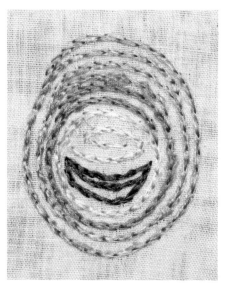

4 Here is an expanded stitch diagram of the peacock eye, showing clearly the way that the shapes of colour overlap at the top only, to build out into an egg shape.

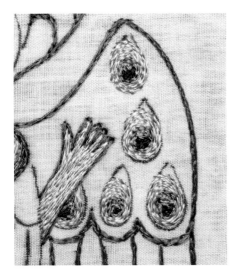

5 Complete the eyes with dark cream, again using the overlap at the top, as shown above. Use two or three layers of cream to build the shape out until it looks about the right size. But, don't worry about exactly filling the teardrop that you have drawn on the canvas: that was really there to just mark the right area. Getting a good shape is far more important to the overall composition than slavishly following a drawn line.

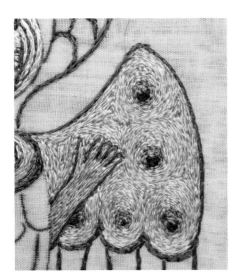

8 Next, fill the leftover spaces with the same colour. Try wherever possible to work in the same direction as the stitching of the established spirals until all of the gaps are filled.

This way of working the peacock wing gives a subtle impression of feather shapes as the light reflects off of the silk. It is a variation of the technique used to dapple the king's horse in The Three Kings project (*see* Chapter 11).

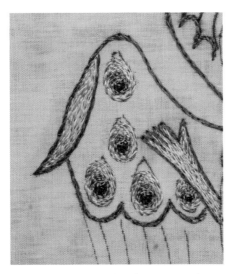

6 Both of the main wings have peacock eyes, but the one on the left-hand side as we look at the embroidery (the cherub's right) has an extra feather flicking out from the top. Some wings in opus have these extra feathers, and some don't, and I don't think that they have any particular significance beyond the personal style of the artist. Include an extra feather, or not – it is your choice. I tend not to, because it often makes the wings look a little clumsy: they stick out to the side too much for my liking.

The extra feather can be filled either with a flat colour (I have used turquoise again) or with a bit of underside couching.

Once your peacock eyes are complete, there are several different ways to fill the wing background. I am showing two here, and a third wing-background option is included in the Rumpelstiltskin project (*see* Chapter 13).

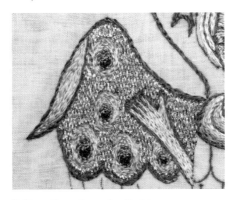

9 The other alternative that I am demonstrating here is to entirely fill the space around the eyes with underside couching. For filling a space such as this one, the basic brick pattern would always be used.

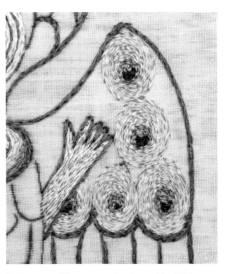

7 You can fill a peacock wing with silk in a colour to contrast with the eyes. Often a pale cream is used to give a relatively subtle effect (if peacock feathers can ever be described as such), akin to the colouring of a white peacock.

I have chosen turquoise to balance the extra feather on the other peacock wing, but teal would also work very well.

Begin by picking up the spiral around each eye, working outwards until the edge touches something.

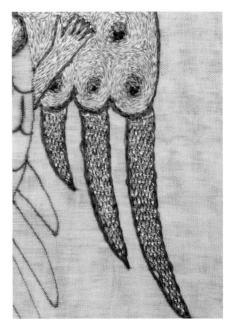

10 You can also use underside couching to fill the long flight feathers on the wings, as shown. I have used it on the right-hand wing to balance the underside couching on the left wing.

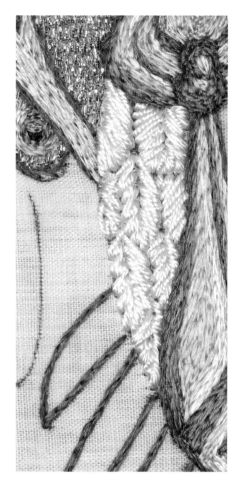

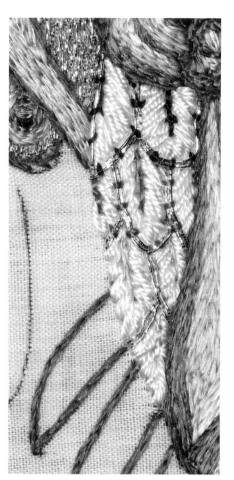

11 I have used the blanco Como silk for working the left-hand-side (his right) body-hugging wing, because I want to balance the white colour used on the wing around the cherub's head. Feathered underside couching packed together like this gives a great deal of texture, but you can easily see why the spines and outlines are needed to add definition.

12 I have kept to the medieval aesthetic by using layers of colour on the white wing, starting with purple at the top and working down through teal, turquoise and light blue. With each colour, I have couched four strands with the same colour for the spines, then used a double row of silver passing thread for the feather outlines, couched down with the same colour as used for the spine of each feather.

13 To finish this wing, I have worked the flight feathers with plain metal-thread underside couching, by using the same silver passing as the surface thread.

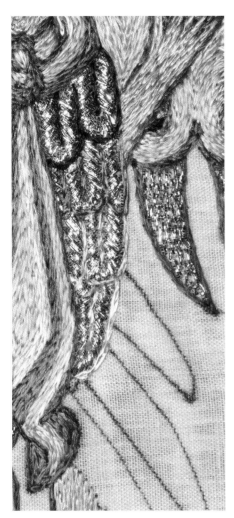

14 The final body-hugging wing features the same feathered-underside-couching technique, but this time done with silver passing thread instead of Como silk. To echo the other wing of the pair, I have graded the outlines and central spines through purple, teal, turquoise and light blue in the same sequence, but this time with the outline and spine of each feather worked with a single, solid colour.

15 At this point, I am going to remove the cherub from the frame and mount him as a slip (*see* Chapter 15), because the feathered underside couching for the long flight feathers of the main peacock-patterned wing on the left-hand side (his right) will look better if worked directly on to the velvet background.

16 Once he has been slipped on to the velvet, I need to mark the location of the flight feathers on the lower right (his left). On any other velvet, I would do such marking by rubbing the velvet the wrong way with a pin, to leave a temporary scar, but this velvet has a very short nap, so I have marked the centre of each feather with a long tacking stitch instead.

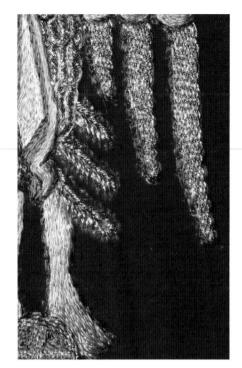

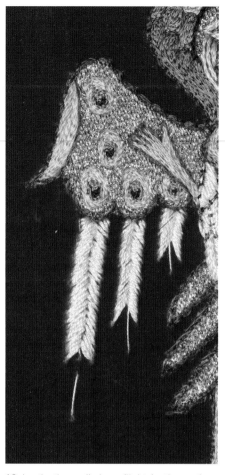

17 These flight feathers are done with the same feathered-underside-couching technique as used for the feathers over the body, but you have to take care to keep the longer edges consistently straight. Start with the diagonal rows of flight feathers because they are shorter and therefore easier. I have worked a simple line of teal down the spine of each feather, but, because I like the feathery edge, I haven't outlined them.

18 Lastly, the really long flight feathers of the main peacock-patterned wing on the left-hand-side (his right) need to be worked. My original plan had been to do these in the same white Como silk as used for the short feathers on the body-hugging wing on this side, but a test patch in the corner of the velvet showed that this particular vintage velvet wasn't robust enough for such a thick thread; instead, I have gone down to using an ecru 30/2nm silk. It is always a good idea to test in this manner, but Como silk would be fine with the majority of velvets. However, if you wanted to, you could also do the short feathers with the 30/2nm thread, to keep these feathers looking all the same.

As before, I marked the position and length of the feathers with a tacking stitch, but, in this case, I am taking the ecru only about two-thirds of the way down each feather.

I have also worked the longest feather slightly differently to the two shorter ones. With a metallic thread, the nature of the thread itself dictates that it be applied by using underside couching, but, when using silk thread for feathers, as here, there is no reason that it couldn't be worked with slanted satin stitch instead of underside couching, since very small areas of satin stitch are used as a feature from time to time in opus. Here, for demonstration purposes, the smaller two feathers are done with satin stitch, and it does give a better finish with the silk, as well as being considerably quicker to do.

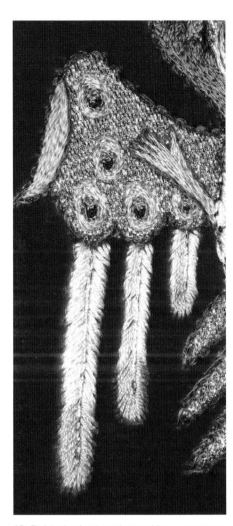

19 Finish the feathers by working a contrast at the ends; I have used a very subtle sky blue in the same 30/2nm weight of silk as used before for the rest of these feathers and then surface couched a double row of silver passing for the spines.

A more dramatic colour contrast would work well with a stronger colour palette, or you could work a metal thread at the end of a coloured one, and you could even shade gold into silver. There are endless variations to be played with!

20 My version is always going to be a little lopsided, but I think that is part of this cherub's charm, and now I have a permanent reminder of all the possibilities for angel's wings.

This is one of those stitch variations that you don't notice at first, but, trust me, once you know about it, you will start noticing it all over the place. I find this stitch quite tricky to work: it is difficult to keep the angle right, and it is easy to mess up the corners, but it is worth persevering with because it does look good once it is done and adds great texture. Plus, you can always take comfort in the fact that many of the original examples are a bit rough around the edges as well.

Mostly this stitch was originally worked with metal thread, but there are examples with silk too, and you may find it easier to start with the silk – it is more forgiving when you pull it out. It is wise to start with working a trial feather off to the side somewhere before plunging into the main image, because this will help you to work out the proper angle of slope of the stitching. I find the hard part is, firstly, to get the initial slope of the feather right and, secondly, to keep it steep enough throughout. It should be a bit shallower than 45 degrees, which I think is part of the problem, because 45 degrees is three-quarters, and three-quarters is sort of a default piece of geometry for the human brain, and your brain keeps trying to slide the stitches back to that angle.

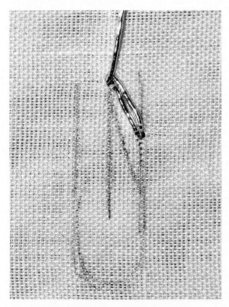 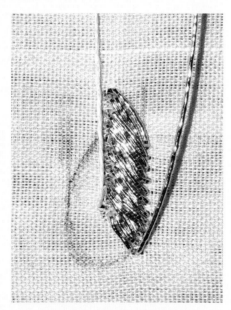 

1 It is best to mark the middle and edge of your feather, and you may find it helpful to mark the angle as well, because it should be quite steep, as shown here. As discussed above, the steep angle is difficult to maintain, and it is easy to wander off into a shallower slope from which it is quite difficult to return. So for very long feathers, you may need a series of markings to keep you on track, but for these little, stubby feathers marking once should suffice.

Start as close to the top of the feather as you can while making a full span of the feather. Don't worry about the short stitches at the feather top for now. All you need to do is to work single underside-couching stitches at an angle, back and forth, as shown.

2 Work down the length of the feather in this manner. Because the couching stitches are longer than is normal, without any interim couching, they will crowd and bunch together far more easily than usual. Try spacing out the stitches a little more if this happens, but you can always burnish the stitches once you finish, by rubbing them with something smooth (this is supposed to be what a mellor is for, but the handle of a small pair of embroidery scissors or a teaspoon works just as well).

3 This is one instance when loops at the back of your underside couching aren't such a big worry; as long as you keep tension on the linen couching thread, the loops will be held tight as you go back and forth.

 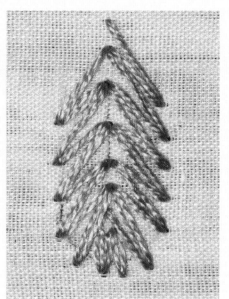 

4 Work around the tip of the feather and up the other side, still working the stitching back and forth. You will be using the holes along the central line of the feather again, so don't pull too hard or you risk tearing the fabric. It can be tricky to get the stitching angle correct on the way up the other side of the feather, but, as long as there is a reasonable slope, it doesn't have to be a mirror image of that of the opposite feather barb. Once you have filled the main body of the feather, you can go back and fill in the top corners. Often, you need to do this only for the top row of feathers; because the feather rows overlap, the tops of the feathers of the lower rows are naturally covered by subsequent feathers.

5 Here is an expanded stitch diagram to illustrate how the stitches need to be shortened at the feather tip to avoid bunching of the stitches.

6 In original pieces with feathered underside couching, there is always a spine down the middle of the feather, and very often the whole feather is outlined as well, especially if you have a lot of feathers packed closely together, as the cherub does for his body-hugging wings. Split stitch or stem stitch will work for this purpose if you use a small needle to slide through the gap in the middle of the feather (though it will be tight), but couched silk is quite commonly used for original pieces – probably because this involves fewer stitches having to be forced in between tightly packed, and easily damaged, metal threads.

I have illustrated using a silk thread couched with a contrasting colour of silk, which seems busy to modern eyes but which is based on usage in original pieces.

CHAPTER 9

THE REAPER

TECHNIQUES

Coloured passing, drapery, skeleton, stones

I wanted to include a small project using modern coloured passing threads, to show the potential for using opus anglicanum in a more contemporary way. The Grim Reaper is my own design based on medieval depictions of skeletons, for no better reason than that I was having a bit of a goth moment.

He is a quick project to complete compared with some of the others, with fun touches of coloured passing to… I want to say liven him up, but that seems like a bit of an oxymoron, so let's say it makes him more interesting, shall we?

He may be quick to sew, but he will certainly challenge you if you choose to mount him as a slip (*see* Chapter 15), since he has lots of wobbly edges.

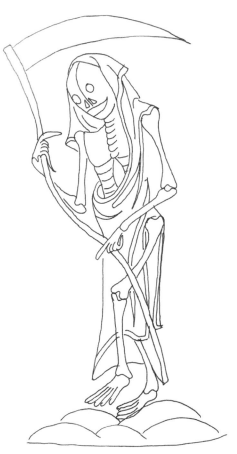

Materials

Fabric
- Double layer of fine ramie or linen fabric (60 to 80 count), 30cm × 30cm (about 12in × 12in)

Needles
- Size 6 crewel needle
- Size 18 chenille needle

Threads
- Silk-filament DeVere Yarns 6 thread, one 200m reel each in the following shades:
  - 44 black ebony
  - 48 crystal/white
  - 71 cappuccino/pale brown
  - 81 acorn/warm brown
  - 101 blanche/cream
  - 118 armour/dark grey
  - 147 solder/mid grey
    Please note that one whole reel of each colour is more than adequate for the working of this project: any thread remaining can be used for the working of several other projects.
- Benton & Johnson smooth passing no 7, one 50m spool each in the following shades:
  - black
  - navy blue
  - red
  - silver
    Please note that one whole spool each of smooth passing is more than adequate for the working of this project: any passing thread remaining can be used for the working of several other projects.
- Strong linen thread, for couching
- Lacing thread

Additional materials
- Beeswax, for waxing linen thread

STEP-BY-STEP INSTRUCTIONS

1 Transfer your design on to the canvas.

2 He is the Grim Reaper: black is very much his colour, so let's start with that. Here, we are going to use black for both the outline and the deepest parts of the shadows.

Be careful to really pack your stitches closely together, because sewing any dark colour on a pale background means that any gaps, however small, will show.

Tip

These robes are depicted in a more naturalistic fashion than for the figures seen so far in the book, so shading of the black areas involves more tapering and flaring out than for the straight lines of the Riggisberg Lady's robes.

As with the Syon Cope project (*see* Chapter 7), there are gaps left that will eventually be filled with ribbons of underside couching, so take care to make these of an even width, so that you can fill them easily when the time comes.

5 Use the brightest white that you have for his teeth; here, I have used crystal. Very small areas of satin stitch are found from time to time in opus anglicanum, usually either when the area is too small to bother with splitting a stitch or when a very high sheen is needed. Work his grin with vertical satin stitch; don't be tempted to go horizontally – we want the light to reflect off his teeth the way that it would off real ones. Plus, a horizontal span of stitching would be too wide and unstable.

Add a few bars of black through the white to delineate his teeth. I think that the teeth look better if they are a bit wonky – and don't worry about the edges being perfect either, as we can tidy that up at the next stage.

3 The middle layer of grey, armour, is used quite thickly to keep the robes dark. Simply follow the lines of the black and work out from there, always remembering to split out of and into the previous stitching layers.

Fill in the lower parts of the cobblestones around his feet, leaving space for highlights.

4 Fill the rest of his robes with solder/mid grey, remembering to leave the spaces for later underside couching. I had originally intended to leave space for highlights of an even paler grey, but the solder is much shinier than the black and dark grey, so it adds its own highlights by bouncing the light around.

Add a highlight layer to both the front and back cobblestones by using this colour.

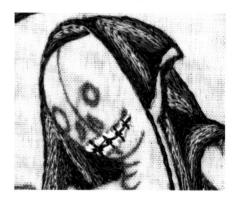

6 Put a bar of black across the middle of the satin-stitch stitching, to finish creating his teeth. You can either work a row of split stitch or surface couch a row as you would for gold thread. I have gone for surface couching, because it adds a more irregular look.

Teeth

The manner of stitching the teeth of our reaper not only creates a deliciously deathly grin but also a probably more authentic arrangement. Bee Wilson, in her book *Consider the Fork*, cites studies showing that the overbite is a modern phenomenon that comes along with the adoption of use of the fork in the West (and it goes back even further in the East, where chopsticks have long been used), before which the standard way of eating was to grip one's bread or meat between the front teeth and cut a piece off with a knife. Hence, the teeth of early European skeletons line up perfectly in this biting grip, which became superfluous with the adoption of forks.

7 Next, we can start on his body, stitching with acorn/warm brown. Medieval skeletons tend to be emaciated cadavers rather than the bleached-white bones of modern cartoons; they have shreds of flesh to hold them together – which makes more sense if, like me, you have an extremely literal imagination and always wonder how the skeletons in *Clash of the Titans* manage to stand up with no connective tissue.

This is why you have a large oval hole in the middle of his torso: it is an opening in his withered flesh, showing the shadow of his empty abdomen, and the mummified skin has stretched tight, revealing his ribs – this hole needs to be filled in with stitching. For his limbs, all you really need to do is add an outline to each bone, but, on his torso, he will need a bit more shadow near the edges of his cloak.

You can also fill in the remaining two cobblestones.

8 Medieval skeletons tend to be a bit brown, so add a layer of shading to the bones by using cappuccino/pale brown. Keep using four strands for the long bones, but switch to using two strands for the skull.

There isn't really room to outline each long bone completely, so I have shaded along just one side and around the joints. Take care to shade along the right-hand side of each bone so that it looks like the light is coming from the left – if you shade some from the left and others from the right, it will be visually confusing. I have also added much deeper shadows to the ribs on the right of his torso.

I have worked three full circles of cappuccino stitching around each eye, to add depth to the orbital sockets, but I kept the shading down to one or two rows of stitching for the rest of the skull.

9 Fill in the rest of his body by using four strands of blanche/cream. Remember to follow the direction of the previously worked stitches and to always split out of or into the previous row.

10 Go down to using two strands for his skull. There isn't as much modelling to do as on a conventional face, because medieval skulls are really just balls with eyes and a mouth, so follow the flow of the shading that you put around the orbital sockets as part of the previous layer of stitching and spiral this new stitching out to create a round shape.

   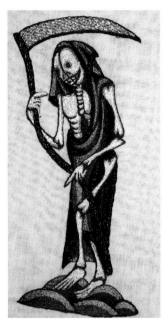

11 The underside couching on his robes was originally going to be purple, for a properly goth look, but it looked a bit too 'disco death' and I picked it out. You should never be afraid to change your mind about a colour or to change it to personalize a design. I have gone for a deep-navy-blue passing instead, which has a bit of sparkle, but which is also a bit more grim and grumpy than is the bright purple.

These are very narrow strips of underside couching, but there are a couple of places where you have to go around corners, which can be challenging. Just make sure to couch down right into the corner, just as you would when cornering split stitch.

12 Add some black smooth passing for the handle of his scythe next. Normally, for conventional opus anglicanum, you would always work underside couching either straight up and down or from side to side, but this is an original design so we are allowed to play a bit fast and loose with the rules and work diagonally and around a curve, so just follow the shape of the handle.

13 Work the silver passing on a diagonal to accentuate the sweep of the scythe blade above his head.

14 Add a tiny spot of red passing to his eyes as the final ghoulish touch.

CHAPTER 10

THE SMALL KNIGHT

TECHNIQUES

Horse, silk underside couching, stem stitch, underside couching, working directly on to a coloured background

I am not sure that this knight is strictly opus anglicanum as such, since he is made entirely of underside couching, with none of the expressive split stitch that is so distinctive of the style: he is maybe more of a precursor. However, he is a great project for getting to grips with underside couching, and it is good experience to try working straight on to a background cloth other than linen. Many later pieces use underside couching very heavily for both robes and background, as we explored with the St Michael and the Dragon project based on part of the Syon Cope (*see* Chapter 7).

He is based on an English fragment from the late twelfth century, and this early date is reflected in the naive style of drawing, which has its own particular charm. He also features both silver and gold metal threads, as well as underside-couched silks, to introduce some more colour.

I am grateful to Dr Timothy Dawson for his advice about medieval horses. The rear end of the horse is missing from the original fragment, so I have had to restore his bum, and I was tempted to give him one of those frilly bum straps that you see in Pre-Raphaelite paintings, but Timothy told me those weren't in use in the twelfth century – he also said that they are called rump straps, which I didn't know. He also told me those bumps on the horse's feet

aren't badly drawn hooves but are instead heavy-duty shoes.

The silk threads that I am using for this project are plied, rather than being the flat filament silks used for the other projects, because flat silks don't work very well for underside couching. The silks used on the original were also plied, which makes sense, because I suspect that twisted silks have always been easier to get hold of, as well as being far easier to work with. I have

used some of the same Como silk that we use pulled apart for other projects in this book, as well as some 30/2nm weaving silks that are quite handy for sewing (DeVere Yarns 36 thread can be used as an alternative, but they are a little thinner). My 30/2nm brown thread is one that I have naturally dyed. However, a similar colour is readily available as aniline-dyed silk.

As well as the usual two layers of fine ramie or linen, this project uses a layer of twill silk. Twill refers to the weave structure of the silk, which is two threads over two, instead of the more basic one over one (known as a tabby weave). Twills are generally more robust than are tabbies (it is quite hard to rip a twill, because the weave structure doesn't give an easy tear line such as you would get with a tabby fabric) so are better able to withstand the punishment of underside couching. Silk taffeta is a tabby weave, but note that it can be a bit temperamental with certain types of embroidery and really isn't ideal for underside couching.

Materials

Fabrics
- Double layer of fine ramie or linen fabric (60 to 80 count), 20cm x 30cm (about 8in x 12in)
- A piece of red twill silk of about the same size as the double-layer ramie or linen fabric, as the top layer of the silk–ramie (or – linen) canvas

Needles
- Size 6 crewel needle
- Size 18 chenille needle
- Como silk thread, one 10g spool in blue
  Please note that one whole spool is more than adequate for the working of this project: any thread remaining can be used for the working of several other projects (for example, for a different-shade bluebird for the Rapunzel project – see Chapter 12).
- 30/2nm spun-silk thread (DeVere Yarns 36 thread will also work), one 10g spool each in the following shades:
  - brown
  - ecru
    Please note that one whole spool of each colour is more than adequate for the working of this project: any thread remaining can be used for the working of several other projects.
- Benton & Johnson smooth passing no 5, up to 10m (about 33ft) each in the following shades:
  - silver
  - dark gold
- Strong linen thread, for couching
- Lacing thread

Additional materials
- Beeswax, for waxing linen thread

STEP-BY-STEP INSTRUCTIONS

1 To prepare for stitching, I first ironed all three layers of fabric quite flat, pinned them, and then ran around the edges with a heavy zigzag-type stitch on the sewing machine, to ensure that everything behaved during the lacing process. Next, transfer the design on to the triple-layer, silk-topped canvas.

Matching colours

I haven't listed black for this project; the brown silk that I have used for the dark stitching was naturally dyed and is actually a sort of purply-grey brown that reads as black against the red. The corresponding stitching of the original is more of a brown, but it could have faded in the last 800 years or so. I never worry about matching the colours of an original piece exactly, because fading has almost certainly taken place over time; it is better to use a shade or two brighter or darker to recreate the original look rather than perpetuate the fallacy that everything in the past was brown.

2 Work the areas of underside-couched silk first, just as you would with a more conventional piece that includes split stitch.

A whole strand of blue Como silk is used for the saddlecloth, couched vertically on to the traced image. This is done in a standard brick pattern, but, instead of spacing the weave over single threads, the saddlecloth is worked as two layers at a time. Two passes of silk are lined up with the holes of identical spacing and then the next two rows are staggered. This gives a much deeper indentation than one-over-one weaving and adds a lovely texture to the cloth. It is great to practice this with silk, as it is much trickier to do it with metal threads.

3 The finer 30/2nm silk is used for the next stage, and only one strand is used.

Use a basic brick pattern to fill the harness, detail on the helmet and the horseshoes. For the original, it is hard to tell whether the underside couching of the reins follows the same direction of stitching as that of the saddlecloth, so I have taken the easy route and worked in the easiest – long – direction, which allowed me to start below the shield, work along the strap, up the bit and along the bridle. For the horseshoes, I worked in the same vertical direction as for the saddlecloth.

Since you have the correct colour of silk in your hand, you might as well use some of it to stitch the eyes in stem stitch (*see* the accompanying 'Stem stitch' box).

4 Add just a tiny bit of underside-couched ecru for the flesh of his face and the stripe on his helmet. There is evidence that helmets of this date were painted, usually with colours corresponding to the relevant heraldry of the wearer, so that is probably what the stripe represents.

While you have some ecru threaded in the needle, you might as well fill in the whites of the eye for both horse and rider. Big, round goggle eyes are typical of this period, but I love how the knight looks as though he has had one too many espressos, and the horse is just rolling his eyes at his foolish rider.

❧ STEM STITCH ☙

As for split stitch, stem stitch is a variation on backstitch, but it works better with a plied thread and creates a slightly raised rope of stitching. Stem stitch appears to be one of the most ancient stitches, used on Iron Age and Viking textiles in Europe, as well as for outlining on the Bayeux Tapestry. Modern embroidery makes a distinction between stem stitch and outline stitch, based on the position of the working thread, but, to me, it is a confusing distinction because, if you rotate the work by 180 degrees, they are the same thing! I sincerely doubt that medieval embroiderers made any such distinction.

1 Start with making a small stitch of about 4mm in length, by bringing the needle from the back to the front of the work and then to the back again. Next, from the back, come up halfway along this stitch – so far this is exactly the same as for split stitch, but... don't split the stitch: instead, push it to one side and come up next to it.

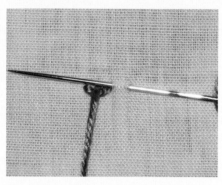

2 The second stitch is of the same length as the first, but, because of the overlap, it advances only half as far along the stitching line. Be sure to place the second stitch down on the same stitching line as for the first, to create an overlap rather than a stagger. If you like, rather than taking the needle fully down when finishing a stitch and then bringing it up again to start a new stitch, angle the needle horizontally as shown and push up the needle tip from the back, to allow you to finish one stitch and start the next stitch in one go.

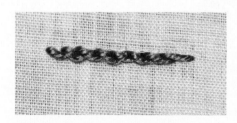

3 Continuing to stitch gives a length of stitching with a ropelike appearance rather than the smooth, flat line characteristic of split stitch. This added dimension is great when you want to make a more pronounced outline.

Always place your new stitch to the same side of the previously made stitch to achieve an even look.

4 As for split stitch, the back of stem stitch should look like a neat row of backstitch.

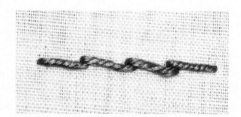

5 As with split stitch, avoid the temptation to go faster by overspacing the stitches and not going all of the way back to halfway along the previously made stitch. The results will be just as messy as if doing this with split stitch.

In all other respects – for spacing, corners, circles, and so on – stem stitch is used in the same way as is split stitch.

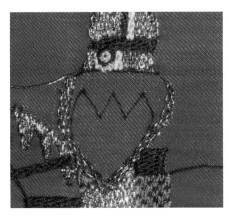

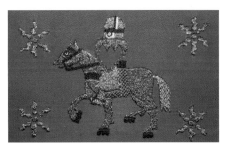

5 Use a plain brick arrangement for the underside-couched silver. I have chosen to do the rays of the stars with silver, but I have reserved the central circle to be done with dark gold, for contrast.

Note that I have also worked the silver on our knight's leg as separate to that of his tunic. There is no shaping here, so delineating the areas of stitching by leaving a gap is important. The final step will be to add definition to these lines with stem stitch.

6 His shield is one of the rare examples where underside couching has been worked around a curve rather than as a straight up-and-down fill.

Start on the outer edge and work inwards in rows until all of the lower edge is filled.

7 Once you have filled the top of his shield, you can continue with working the rest of the horse with the same dark gold. Again, as with the knight, take care to work around the lines where his legs cross over one another. He is really quite flat, and the lines are the only thing that add some definition to him.

He is getting to be a very sparkly pony by this point, and the red–gold contrast makes it hard to focus.

8 The final step is to outline with stem stitch. I haven't outlined the underside couching on the star, partly because I can see no sign of outlining on the original and partly because it looks better with a raw edge. The rest of the piece is outlined with brown along the sides of the gold, ecru outside the blue and silver, and blue along the brown.

It is not the easiest job to outline alongside the gold threads; you just have to try to slide under and between them, so take your time, and take care not to pierce any of the metal threads as you go.

CHAPTER 11

THE THREE KINGS

TECHNIQUES

Basket-weave background, underside couching, columns, dapples, fur, ground, horses

A full size template for the basket-weave back ground is given in the Appendix.

Materials

Fabric
- Double layer of fine ramie or linen fabric (60 to 80 count), 46cm x 46cm (about 18in by 18in)

Needles
- Size 7 crewel needle
- Size 18 chenille needle

Threads
- Silk-filament DeVere Yarns 6 thread, one 200m reel each in the following shades:
  - 01 white
  - 03 lemon/yellow
  - 45 green
  - 53 foil/silver
  - 55 beeswax/warm yellow
  - 57 star/pale blue
  - 60 eggshell/pale brown
  - 71 cappuccino/pale brown
  - 73 cosmos/very dark blue
  - 75 freshwater/bright blue
  - 104 avocado/very dark green
  - 108 capsicum/bright green
  - 122 apple/pale green
  - 137 cigar/very dark brown
  - 141 denim/mid blue
  - 181 allspice/warm brown
  - 228 nut/mid brown
  - 243 cactus/dirty green
  - 620 fresh apple/very pale green
  - i90 ingot/gold
    Please note that one whole reel of each colour is more than adequate for the working of this project: any thread remaining can be used for the working of several other projects.
- Benton & Johnson smooth passing no 5, in the following shades:
  - silver (at least 5m, or about 16½ft)
  - very dark gold (at least 5m, or about 16½ft)
  - white gold (one 50m spool)
- Strong linen thread, for couching
- Lacing thread

Additional materials
- Beeswax, for waxing linen thread

This panel is based on The Three Magi from the Bologna Cope (AD1310–20). I have chosen it so that we can look in detail at portraying animals, specifically horses, which are by far the most common beasts featured in opus anglicanum. However, the techniques used to depict horses can easily be transferred to other creatures, from dogs to dragons, as the methods used to depict the musculature and faces are quite similar. The foremost horse is a lovely example of dappling, which is great fun to do, and this is also a technique commonly used to depict the ground, so it is a versatile and useful thing to learn.

I will admit that one of my other main reasons for choosing this particular image is the fact that the brown horse is just plain silly. He is giving one of the finest examples of medieval side-eye that I have ever seen, and I can never resist a good, funny look – that horse couldn't be looking dafter if he was wearing a traffic cone on his head.

We will also look at using underside couching to create more complex background patterns than the simple chevrons featured on the Syon Cope.

1 Transfer the design on to your canvas. You need to be quite careful with this design, as it has a lot of legs in it. It can be decidedly irritating when you have spent hours transposing a medieval image only to realize that you have drawn seven legs for four people and you can't quite figure out where the eighth leg ought to go or to whom it should be attached. (In fact, having checked back to the original, I think that the legs of this big jumble are in slightly the wrong places on the source material too.)

That said, I always regard the drawing as a guide, rather than as a strict rule, and some areas are more important to transfer accurately then others. In this case, when it comes to the wiggly lines that indicate the ground, accuracy isn't important at all.

2 I am a big fan of beginning with an easy bit, to get myself into the swing of things, so, in this case, start with the stylized architecture of the frame, which is mainly a series of nice straight lines and simple curves. Use between four and six strands of silk filament with the smaller of the two needles; for reference, I have used five strands. In this case, I am not going to outline the whole thing at once but, instead, take one section at a time, because the outline colours are mostly going to be darker shades of those used for filling. I am also going to vary the outline widths, to create shaping and to give the impression that light emanates from the Magi, by putting the darker shadows to the outer edges.

So, for each column, the body of the column is outlined with nut/mid brown, with one line of stitching on the inner edge and two on the outer edge.

The column base, capital, and the inner span of the arch are outlined with cosmos/very dark blue, with some shaping being applied to the base, and two lines of stitching being used for the arch.

The outer arch has two rows of green at the outer edge.

For each of these elements, all the stitching flows in the same direction. One reasonable length of thread is about the right amount for one row of stitching, so, in this case, making everything flow in the same direction is pretty easy.

3 Begin to add some shading to the original outlines. Here, I have used:
- Ingot/gold on the column, three rows being worked along the inner side and six on the outer;
- Denim/mid blue on the column bases, capitals, and inner arch, again with some shaping being used for the capitals, and with three rows being worked for the inner arch;
- Capsicum/bright green for the outer arch, with three rows being worked.

Counting rows

Although I have told you here how many rows of stitching I have used in each case, you shouldn't feel obliged to count your own rows. I am just trying to give you an idea of how I have built up the shading: remember that opus anglicanum is *not* a counted-stitch or -row embroidery technique. Use your eye and your judgement to decide when you have built up enough of each colour to suit *your* taste.

Also, bear in mind that the thickness of thread can vary dramatically; even if you use threads from within the same range, you will find slight variations – when working this project, I found that the denim/mid blue was much thinner than the ingot/gold, even though these two shades are from the same source, so I used six strands of the blue while continuing to use only five of the gold. Do what feels right, and adapt the number of thread strands used as you sew!

4 Next, fill in some of the highlights. The body of the column is basically just colouring in the remaining space with beeswax/warm yellow. As with the rest of the frame, it is easy to keep all of the stitches flowing in the same direction, because one decent sewing length of thread will be sufficient for working about one row.

The inner arch and column are finished with star/pale blue. Again, to give you a rough idea of the depth of shading, I have built up four rows of this colour on the arch.

Finally, the rest of the outer arch is filled with fresh apple/very pale green. My drawing went a little bit wobbly in places, so there wasn't always room for four rows, so I have filled in where the width varies by working an extra row of stitching. If you want your arch to be perfectly even, you could start with the pale green and work outwards, rather than inwards as I have done, but I don't mind a bit of wobble.

5 Start filling in the ground by working the wiggly lines with green. If you want to, you can use a slightly thicker thread for the floor: it is dirt and unlikely to be smooth and perfect. In this case, I have gone from using five strands up to six, because the floor is a bit boring – I would prefer to get it over and done with.

6 Next, fill in the middle colour for the ground. Here, I am using the same capsicum/bright green as used for the outer arch. It is often tempting to use a whole new set of green shades to demarcate a separate area, but, if you look at original pieces, they often have very few shades used in them, which creates a more harmonious look to the finished piece.

How much you fill in at this stage is a matter of personal choice. I have worked roughly four rows at the top and five at the bottom, but you could use more, or less. You are likely to also need to work some triangular stitching (*see* Step 9 of the section 'Three-quarter face' in Chapter 3) here and there, to complete little shapes in the areas to be filled in. There is a natural variation in the thickness of the bright green caused by working around the curves, but you can exaggerate this by using the layering technique previously highlighted (*see* 'The basic stitch: split stitch' in Chapter 2). Remember to always split something: try to always start a new row by coming out of the previous one and end the row by going down into an existing stitch.

7 Finally, fill in the areas of palest green with apple/pale green, again using triangular stitching where needed. I have used a slightly darker green than the lovely silvery shade used on the arch (that thread shade is called fresh apple rather than just plain apple). Using two of the greens already used elsewhere in the piece with this new green not only ties the arch to the base of the image but also creates a sense of weight.

You could instead use the fresh apple/very pale green on the ground here if you wanted to, but, when I put that green on the floor, it looks so pale and clean that I worry about it getting dirty beneath the horse's hooves, and such things can be very jarring to the eye.

8 Next, we will move on to the drapery of our three kings. Because we have already worked through detailed step-by-step instructions for drapery on the single figures of St Lawrence and the Riggisberg Lady, I am going to do the stitching of all three kings at once.

We are going to use the same range of blues, greens and golds as we employed for the arch and ground, which will help to keep the image harmonious, but we will also mix in some new colours. By using a couple of new golds and yellows mixed in with the ones that are already present, we can add new depth and complexity, without jarring the eye too much.

The foremost king has his outer robe outlined with nut/mid brown, and I have included some shading. The sleeve of his under robe is outlined with cosmos/very dark blue, and his leg is outlined with cigar/very dark brown.

The saddlecloth of his horse is outlined with avocado/very dark green, and I have added two separate horizontal rows of stitching here, to indicate where a row of gold will eventually go.

The rearmost king, of whom very little is seen, is outlined with cigar/very dark brown.

The middle king, the one who is gesturing forwards, is outlined with green, and again I have put in some very subtle shading with this thread.

The foremost horse's testicles are also outlined with cigar/very dark brown.

Tip

Mainly, this step is a case of outlining the robes and saddle cloth, but you can add a tiny bit of shading at this point too, as long as you don't overdo it. Remember that these are your outlines and represent the deepest shadows of the robes. You need to leave room for the rest of the colours! So, in some places only, I have used two or three rows of stitching to emphasize shade, but mostly I have just outlined with one row of stitches.

A note about genitalia

If you find equine genitalia distasteful, you can castrate the horse here by leaving his testicles out of the image, although it should be said that animal genitalia of all kinds are pretty ubiquitous in medieval art, even when that art was intended for religious use. I think that the purpose of Dobbin's nuts in this image is mainly to emphasize the fact that his rider is a king, because, to the medieval mind, a king who chooses to ride a mare or gelding would be perceived as lacking in requisite levels of masculinity for a monarch. A stallion is basically the medieval version of a supercar in terms of metaphorical willy-waving. Here endeth the history lesson: your normal sewing service will now resume.

9 The foremost king has ingot/gold applied to his outer robe, denim/mid blue to his sleeve, and nut/mid brown to his leg (and again nut/mid brown to fill in his horse's testicles, again optional). Although the folds of his golden robe are worked in straightish lines, there is a row of extra ingot/gold added towards the bottom of the folds, to shape them slightly. The leg has subtle shaping added, beginning to outline the shape of the thigh and calf by adding a layer of shadow at the back of the knee and thigh.

The saddlecloth of the foremost horse has been partially filled with green. The saddlecloth is flatter than the robes, and more simply depicted, so I have filled in quite a lot already and will use only one more colour to completely fill this area.

The rearmost king's shoulder has been given some shape with nut/mid brown.

The middle king has another layer of shading worked in capsicum/bright green. By working the darker shades to the base of this figure, and the lighter ones to the top, we will give the layering of the three figures a little bit of depth.

10 Next is the penultimate fill of colour. Remember when working this set of colours to leave room for the final – highlighting – colour. In many areas, this will be a barely visible gap that is just wide enough to accommodate one row of stitching.

The foremost king has a layer of beeswax/warm yellow added to his robe and some freshwater/bright blue on his arm. In the original embroidery, his leg is a of very pale buff colour with minimal shading, so I have just worked a single line of ingot/gold here, but you could easily leave this out and work his leg with only two colours.

The saddlecloth of his horse is completely filled with capsicum/bright green.

For the rearmost king, I have also added a thin line of ingot/gold to his robe.

The middle king has a layer of shading worked with capsicum/bright green. There is more shaping to the drapery of the green king than for the other two at this stage, so layer the stitches carefully and remember... always split something.

11 Finally, you can fill in the highlights. The foremost king has his robes finished with a tasteful splash of lemon/yellow, his sleeves with star/pale blue, and his leg with cappuccino/pale brown.

The rearmost king has cappuccino/pale brown stitching added as well. I was originally tempted to make his robes less dull and mousey by shifting his colours from the original browns to a richer, deep red. However, this would have meant introducing a whole new set of colours just for him, and he would have stuck out like the proverbial sore thumb. Keeping him dull means that he doesn't destroy the harmony of the composition, and it is always worth bearing this in mind when thinking about which colours to incorporate.

The rest of the robes of the middle king is filled in with fresh apple/very pale green, which changes the tone of the accompanying capsicum/bright green quite a lot.

Tips

The kings' robes are going to be worked with four layers of colour in total, so, as we lay down the next layer of stitching, we again need to work with a light touch. As mentioned previously, in what proportion you work these layers is very much a matter of personal taste, and you can easily make one colour more dominant by using a thicker layer than I am presenting here.

Remember that, when layering rows of stitches, always split something. Split in and split out, and try to work large areas of stitching in the same direction.

Omissions when tracing

When you are transcribing an original image to embroider, it is quite easy to overlook small details and then find that you need to fill them in later (and I refer you back to what I said about making sure you have the right number of legs). You may, for instance, realize that you have forgotten to draw in the girth that secures the saddle and thus preserves the royal dignity, by making sure that he stays on his horse. Such small details are easy to fill in as you go along; in this case, I am using ingot/gold. Of course, if you happen to be writing an embroidery book at the time, such an oversight is quite embarrassing, so your best bet is to pretend that you did it deliberately to make a point and then nip back and adjust your original drawing so that the reader is none the wiser.

Fur

Apart from prominent horse testicles, one of the other visual indicators of wealth in this image is the fur worn by the kings. This is of a type known as vair, which is basically squirrel pelts that are arranged and patched together so that the white belly fur and darker back fur form a regular pattern. This pattern is used in all forms of medieval art that depict the clothing of the wealthy, where it is mainly seen as a lining for cloaks and gowns, although here it is also worn as a prominent collar in a style usually reserved for kings.

Fur was regulated by sumptuary laws, so your status in society dictated what type of fur you were allowed to wear, and vair was reserved for the nobility. Vair is also used as a pattern in heraldry, because it is associated with nobles. Real vair can vary a lot, but, in art, it is indicated by a distinctive pattern, which we are going to reproduce here.

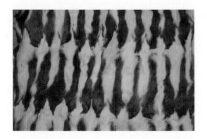

12 In order to map out the vair pattern, I find it easiest to divide the area into a grid, with one square for each portion of pelt. You could do this with a pencil or chalk, but I find it easiest to do it with a single line of stitching of the colour that I will be using for the dark part of the fur – in this case, that is foil/silver. I am still using four strands to work with – the same as for the robes. On his broad collar, this marking out is quite simple, but, on the triangular panels that show the lining of the cloak, you will end up with some irregular shapes. Where only a minute sliver of fur shows inside the cuff, you can't show a whole skin, but, by filling it partly with grey, and partly with white, the eye will fill in the detail.

13 Next, stitch a tongue shape inside each marked square with the foil/silver thread.

14 Continuing to use the foil/silver thread, fill in the grey background. If you are using a stitched grid like I am, you can work over it so that the grey becomes a uniform shade without divisions. Remember to always split something!

Once the grey is filled in, the tongues can be filled in with white. On some depictions of fur, there are two tiny vertical flicks of brown added at the top of each tongue (here I have used ingot/gold just for working the single stitches); other depictions leave out this detail and the pattern is still recognizable as vair, so, whether you include this detail or not is optional.

15 As you can see, once his robe is properly fur-lined, our foremost king looks suitably regal.

16 Outline the faces and all visible hands with four strands of cigar/very dark brown. When you outline the green king's hand, make sure that this outline butts right up against the border (*see* the hand close-up for the following step); this is so that, when you come to working the couched gold background, you don't end up with an awkward fiddly bit between the hand and the border.

Use a touch of colour for the irises, choosing whatever three colours you fancy from the ones already used for the robes, and fill in the whites. I have tried to mix the colours up and give each king an eye colour that is different to what he is wearing, but you can make the eyes any colour you like. Remember to always split out of and into something – this is especially important with the eyes, as they are where the viewer will focus.

17 I always like to do the hands before the faces. No matter how long I work with filament silks, I always find it a bit of a shock to the system to go down to using the thinner threads, so doing the hands and feet first gives me time to adjust. In this case, go down to using two strands of eggshell/pale brown as the flesh colour.

Emphasize the elegant gesture of the green king's hand by taking the filling thread out from his smallest finger and around the base of the back of his hand before going up his index finger, and continue following this stitching course to fill in the upper hand. Next, fill in what can be seen of his lower arm, and taper the threads into his wrist to add a twisting action.

Stitching order

My usual stitching order would be to deal with faces and hands last because they require the use of the finest threads, but, since we have already dealt with faces in previous projects, I am going to take things in order of familiarity for this project and do the horses last. So, the faces are the next step.

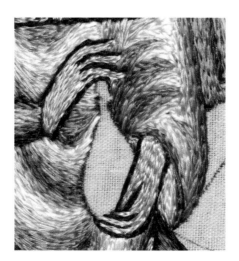

‹**18** Stitching for the foremost king's hands, holding the bottle, is a simple matter of filling in the area with straight lines coming out from his wrist. Keep the flow of his hands by returning to the wrist once you reach the fingertip, so that all of the stitches flow in the same direction.

19 There isn't a lot of shaping that you can put into the kings' necks, because their beards are in the way, so just neatly fill in what can be seen. I am breaking my own rule about always splitting something along their necks, because the rough edges of these split stitches areas will later be covered by the ends of the beards and hair.

20 Fill the apples of the kings' cheeks next. I think that the rearmost king looks younger than the other two, so I have given him nice round apples, but I have tried to make the other two look a bit saggier, because I think they are older. These are quite small faces, though, so there is a limit to how much sag you can work in.

Bonus points if you can make them give each other funny looks, as this will make the whole thing look much more medieval. I think the two at the back, following behind the green king, are exchanging a look because our green king has gone off with the faeries again.

Don't worry about that tiny gap of unfilled canvas on the rearmost king's collar: we will put a dash of gold in there eventually, because he is a dowdy little king and he needs something shiny.

21 Next, fill their foreheads and noses, remembering to work in one direction only – although here you could try going back and forth in a block of three or four rows of stitches, to give a subtle wrinkled effect to the foreheads.

Again, I am breaking my own rule about always splitting out of or into something as I work over the foreheads, because the edges of these blocks of stitching will be obscured by the hair.

22 Fill in the brow areas and assorted little fiddly bits, remembering to always split out and in. Only the rearmost king, seen at the centre, has a proper chin, because he doesn't have a beard; with the other two, you just need to fill in the upper lip because they have beards but no moustaches (which I have always thought is the least attractive of all possible styles of beard, but it seems to have been inexplicably popular in the Middles Ages).

23 The final touch for the faces is to do the hair. For this, I have gone back up to using four strands. You could comfortably change their hair colours to anything you like, and, as long as you choose from the existing palette, it wouldn't disturb the harmony of the image: even green hair isn't unfeasible in terms of medieval imagery, and this piece does include a green horse, after all. However, for the foremost king, I have used cigar/very dark brown and cappuccino/pale brown, for the rearmost king ingot/gold and lemon/ yellow, and, for the middle king denim/mid blue and foil/silver.

Animal faces

Often the faces of animals, just like those of humans, need to be worked with a finer thread – if you look at your pet cat or dog, the hair of their faces is usually shorter and finer than that of their bodies. However, I have chosen to work these horses' faces with four strands because the image is quite large.

Tip

Unlike human faces, the faces of animals are worked with layers of colour in the same way as you would work them for drapery or the body of the beast, but the shading still needs to follow the facial structure.

24 It is time to move on to the horses, and, as usual, we are going to start from the back and work into the foreground: the big green pony is up first. I have no idea why he is green, other than that the original one on the cope is green. Maybe he has gone a bit mouldy from being left in a damp stable, who knows? My best guess is that the original embroiderer had already used brown and both blue and grey for the other two horses, respectively, so just used what was left on hand, regardless of colour.

We are still using four strands of thread here, but, if you want to, you can use just two for working the horse's faces.

We actually don't see that much of the green one, but we will start with outlining him in avocado/very dark green and filling in the iris of his eye with a dab of cigar/very dark brown.

Fill in the hooves with a solid little block of cigar/very dark brown. I refer you to my comments above about there being a lot of legs in this image. I have done the stitching for the hooves of each horse in a slightly different colour, so be careful that you colour code the right hooves to the right horse, because they already look like they are playing twister – it certainly doesn't need to get any more confusing.

Horses

These horses are drawn pretty well by medieval standards – by which I mean that they do indeed look like horses, rather than generic quadrupeds who may or may not have had some of their limbs broken.

Medieval art never seems to present any eye other than human ones, even when representing animals, so you need to leave a good bit of room for the white of the eye here.

You may notice that the green horse is very short backed, which goes back to how badly drawn horses generally are within medieval art; I think that these horses have all been squished a bit to fit the frame – with medieval art, its practitioners always prefer to draw the whole thing rather than let the frame cut something out, so things are often squished.

25 A big, green horse is weird enough, so, to avoid making him even weirder, I have worked him in the muckier shades of green, starting with the same green as used for the darker parts of the ground below. Add some stitching to shade the outer edges of each leg before moving up to his face and neck.

Begin layering some texture for his mane. Play with the waves and texture by varying the number of rows being worked, but always remember to split something to keep the mane flowing smoothly.

As well as a thick stripe to accentuate the shape of his jugular, he needs a broad stripe of shadow at the top of his neck; spacing this a few millimetres down from the mane will help to emphasize the muscles here – horses have very muscular necks, and you want to make his neck look proud and nobly arched. His rider is a king, after all. To bring out the facial form, emphasize the curve of the cheek with some shadow, and give him eyebrows to echo the curve of the bone above a real horse's brow.

26 The next layer is worked in cactus/dirty green, which is a shade that we are going to use only for this horse. Mainly, this shade is used to emphasize and extend the line of dark green laid down by using the previous shade.

Note that the green horse's foremost hoof, the one seen jauntily prancing just behind the brown horse's neck, doesn't have any greens worked into it yet, nor do the lower sections of his other legs.

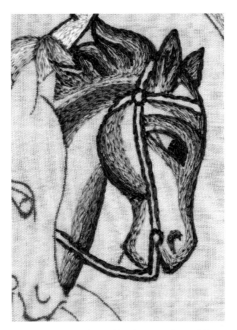

27 This cactus thread is also used to add some extra shading above and below the eye, as shown.

29 The final step for the green horse is to make him look all minty fresh with a few touches of white, by filling in the white of his eye and stitching his little socks (*see also* the following step).

28 Fill in the majority of the rest of his body with apple/pale green. This is the same colour we used for the green king's drapery, but, when contrasted against a different set of greens, it changes its shade quite a lot.

At this point, we are going to venture down into the lower limbs by laying down some shading with this pale shade. Using the colour used to highlight the rest of the body as a shadow on the white hocks will visually tie the two sections of leg together.

Remember, when filling in, to always split something and to follow the direction of stitching of the previously laid-down colours.

30 When working his socks, stitch the white in rows worked down the lower leg from top to bottom, splitting them into the top of the hooves at a right angle. This gives a fair semblance of the way that a real horse's hair lies over the top of the hoof.

31 Working from back to front makes the brown horse next in line. He is my favourite; the other two look like respectable, well-behaved steeds, whereas this chap looks like he is going to go through your pockets for carrots and run away from the halter when you are trying to get him to come in from the paddock. And you can tell by the look on his face that he thinks his rider is an idiot, so you need to place the pupils in the upper quarter of the eye, so that it looks as if he is rolling his eyes at the latest stupid thing his majesty just said.

Start by outlining him with cigar/very dark brown. Again, be careful to attach the correct legs, although this gets easier with fewer horses still to stitch. Also, give him a nice, neat centre parting to his mane.

Fill in his hooves with cappuccino/pale brown, and, because he has no other areas of white, you might as well fill in the whites of his eyes.

Horse faces

Full-frontal-profile faces are really quite rare in medieval art, but they are depicted more frequently for horses than for any other creature, usually with comical results.

32 Shade his body with allspice/warm brown. As with the green horse, he needs a lot of shape and shadow to his neck to make it look muscular

The shading on the legs of all of the horses is conversely very simplistic, giving no emphasis at all to joints or kneecaps. Basically, if a horse's legs look like boneless strands of spaghetti that couldn't possibly hold up a large quadruped, you are probably doing your stitching right — other styles practised by medieval artists when depicting horses include 'hit by a train and then reassembled without referring to the manual' and 'No, actually, I have never before seen this creature that you call a horse'.

By contrast, the shading that shapes his face is pretty accurate, apart from him having those human eyes. Give him dramatic, ancient Egyptian–style eyeliner with a big flick at both ends to emphasize the broad, flat front part of his head and also a little dent at the top just under his bridle, to echo the shape of his ears.

33 Add some shading with nut/mid brown, but be careful not to overdo it: you need to leave room for the highlight colour.

On his face, this layer will join up some of the lines laid down by the previous stitching colour.

Start on his mane, which we didn't touch when working the last layer of colour, layering up from the outline.

34 Use ingot/gold to fill in most of the remaining areas of his body.

Remember, always split something, and work in the same direction as that of the previous stitches.

Add a second layer of colour to his mane. Try to create shapes for the locks of his hair by splitting the ends into clumps (for once, split ends in your hair are going to a be a good thing), but leave room for working a final layer of highlights.

35 Finally, add highlights to his mane by using beeswax/warm yellow.

36 Next up is the blue horse, or maybe he is really a dappled grey. I think that the blue horses in medieval embroidery are a dye problem – it is quite tricky to get good, reliable greys with natural dyes, so they just substituted blue for grey in much the same way that cats are classed as blue when they are, really, grey. Of course, white horses are properly referred to as grey, even when they are snow white, so it is all very confusing. This horse has some blue, some grey, and some white, so you can call him what you like. I am going to stick with blue though.

Outline him with cosmos/very dark blue. At the top of his tail, under his belly, and on his face, to add shape, I have doubled or sometimes tripled the outline, but be careful not to overdo it. And always remember to split out of or into the first outline. He also needs a thick double line of dark blue to emphasize the muscles of his neck, just as for the green horse. And every well-dressed horse needs eyeliner.

I have already discussed his testicles, so let's not go there again.

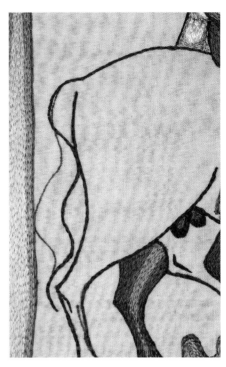

37 When it comes to his tail, it is best to lay down one dominant line before working all of the others, as shown here. His tail is glamorous and swishy, so try to add some interesting curves before doubling that line up and working out from it, leaving plenty of room for working another couple of layers of colour.

38› Add delicate shading with denim/mid blue. This shading needs to be stitched with a much lighter touch than for the other two horses: in most places, just one or two lines are needed, because we need to leave room for the dapples, which are the exciting part. The only places that I have gone up to three rows of this colour are on the thigh and belly, plus a tiny bit of shadow at the top of his foremost leg – the one that's prancing.

He also needs a tiny bit of shading under his eye, which makes him look a bit hung-over, but which also emphasizes his eye.

Add one or two rows of stitching on the mane and tail, depending on space and how dark you want them to be. Work down the tail and up the mane: you basically want to stitch in the direction that the hair would naturally grow.

Remember, always split something.

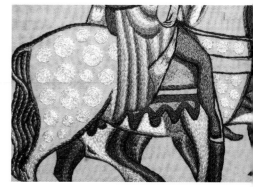

39 The next layer of shading is done with freshwater/bright blue. Again, keep it light and delicate for the upper body, but layer the stitching to fill the lower legs completely below the knee (or at least where the knees would be if the original scribe was better at drawing horses). Don't just cut a straight line across the leg as if he is wearing blue socks, instead fan out the stitches to make a downward-facing V-shape, which looks more natural.

This blue is the final layer of colour for the mane and tail, which should by now look swishy and bouncy, because this horse clearly spends all of his pocket money on conditioner.

He needs a touch of eyeshadow and some shading for his ears and upper neck, but, apart from the belly, he doesn't need much blue on the majority of his body.

40 We will use some white next, still working with four strands.

Fill his face by working around the cheek area until it is full, and then work up his nose and around the eye. In this case, you don't have to go around the back to maintain a unified direction of stitching, because you can work the cheek and nose as a circuit by just ducking under the bridle where necessary. The areas to be filled model the basic shape of the face.

Also fill the upper neck between the mane and line of muscle, the belly, and each of the legs with solid white. As with the blue of the previous layer, work a sort of V-shape between the upright part of the foremost hind leg and the haunches.

41 And now for the exciting part – dapples. There are actually two kinds of dapples on this horse, and we are starting with the slightly more complicated sort, filling the haunches, forequarters and the little area between the two pieces of harness.

You can work in from the edge as you would when working the cheek of a face, but this involves having faith that you can stitch an almost perfect circle. This is the method that I used at the top of the haunch, and, if you look carefully at the large blob second from left on the top row, you will see a little tail sticking out where I misjudged the angle. The tail isn't really a problem – you can just sew over it when working the next layer of stitching. Nor is it a problem if your blobs aren't all perfect circles, because the image is of an organic object that would naturally contain some variation.

Try to work all of the dapple circles in the same direction. To be honest, most people tend to instinctively work consistently either clockwise or anticlockwise, so it is probably not something that you will need to think about much. It is not the end of the world if you randomly make one anticlockwise blob amongst twenty clockwise ones, but it is easier to fill in the gaps between the dapples if they all spiral in one direction.

Leave a 4mm to 5mm gap between each blob, and don't try to make them all of the same size. They should be larger or smaller to fit into the available space and be just as varied as the dapples on a real horse.

Tip

There is no right or wrong pattern in which to lay down the circles that fill these areas; it is best to treat it organically – put one circle down in a corner and let it grow from there. Trying to follow an exact pattern would drive you nuts, but, if you want to sketch a few rough circles on to the canvas as a guide first, that is OK – it is best to use either a permanent ink that you know won't bleed or wash out or a coloured tailor's chalk. I really wouldn't recommend pencil in this instance, in case the graphite later rubs off on the white silk and makes it grubby.

All in all, it really is best to just take a deep breath and go for it, without any marking out beforehand at all.

DAPPLING METHODS

Here, I am presenting two effective methods for working dapples. Using either method is fine, and I suggest that you try both and see which you prefer.

Method one: outer edge first

Method two: working out from the centre

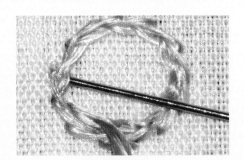

Here, I am showing a two-colour version of the dapple circle to demonstrate how each of the inner rows layers up. Remember to bite into the outer row with the inner one to get good stitch coverage.

Alternatively. you can work three tiny satin stitches at the centre of your circle and spiral out from that, as demonstrated here.

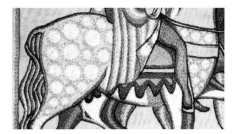

42 We will use four strands of freshwater/bright blue next.

Split out of each individual white circle and work outwards, following the direction of the core and spiralling around it. There isn't a rule of how many times you should go around each blob – in my case, it was usually three or four. What you want to end up with is the outer blue rings just touching each other, or touching the side of the haunch, but without any one ring taking visual dominance. If your blobs are in an irregular layout, it is enough to work until each blob touches something, but it doesn't have to touch all of its dapple neighbours – to achieve this, you would have had to lay them down in a precise grid, which would look unnatural and forced.

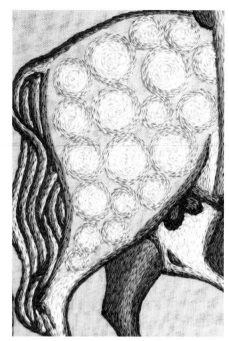

43 I have included this close-up of this dapple stitching to help you to see how the elements of the stitching interact. Don't worry about the irregularity of the gaps between the blobs!

‹**45** The neck features dappling of one colour to create a much more subtle textured effect. It is hard for a photograph to really do justice to how perfectly this technique exploits the sheen of the silk; you really have to see the cloth moving in sunlight. On a medieval bishop's cope, it would have caught the light just as much as did the gold threads. Again, we are so used to seeing opus anglicanum close up, in photographs or with our noses pressed up against the display case in the V&A, that we forget that it was typically seen from a distance in the candlelit gloom of a great Gothic cathedral as the clergy processed by in all their pomp. The way that the light dances on the silk was just as much a part of the glamour as the glitter of gold.

So, it is white only for this section, and, whereas before we left deliberate gaps between the circles, this time the dapples need to be packed as tightly together as possible.

As before, try not to make the circles too regular.

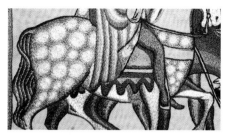

44 Complete the dappling by using four strands of foil/silver to fill in all of the gaps between the dapples. I find that it is best to be as systematic as possible here, to avoid missing anything. I worked from the top right of the haunch, just under the saddle, following the blue shading down the rump edge, where there is still a slice of empty space, all of the way down until I hit something, then I used the end of the strand to fill the small adjacent spaces, finished off, and then went back up to the starting position and repeated this two or three times until the left-hand spaces were all filled. Then I did the same down the other side, before working my way up through the gaps.

Always work along the edges of the circles, continuing the outward spiral wherever possible. Often, you will find yourself following the edge of the circle between tight gaps to fill every tiny space.

You will find yourself making ample use of little areas of triangular stitching that we employed to fill spaces in the grass (again, as introduced in Chapter 3). Again, remember to always split something.

46 Next, fill in all of the gaps with the same white. To be honest, if I wasn't doing this for demonstration, I would fill in these gaps as a I went along. White on white is tricky to work and it is easy to miss a bit, so filling in as you go makes sense.

I have worked his neck in white, as the original was done, and it does look a little odd, even in the original, especially as the reins make such a severe cut-off point and division between the multicoloured and single-colour areas of dappling. It is a perfectly valid interpretation do treat the neck in the same multicoloured way as used for the rest of the body, if you prefer.

47 Some basic underside couching is required for working the harnesses, using just the most basic brick arrangement for the stitches, or a diagonal if you are feeling adventurous. I have used silver passing for the grey horse and very dark gold passing for the other two horses, and also for the jar of myrrh held by the foremost king. It would be an equally valid choice to use the same white gold passing thread that will later be used for the background to work all of the harnesses, but the contrast is better using varied shades, and, as we saw for The Small Knight project (*see* Chapter 10), it is a perfectly period choice to use different couching shades.

If you have kept your rows of split stitching nice and close together for the reins, you shouldn't need more than three rows of couching to fill them, so it is a relatively quick job.

Remember to use the larger crewel needle for this couching step and to wax the linen thread.

48 The breast band of the blue horse is slightly more detailed. Use the same capsicum/bright green as used for his saddlecloth and the cosmos/very dark blue that he is outlined with to make an alternating band of satin stitch across the middle of the band. This isn't cheating by introducing an unorthodox stitch, because, although satin stitch isn't a huge part of opus anglicanum, it is occasionally used for tiny areas such as this, where it gives a jewel-like lustre. It is, though, never used for large areas, only for tiny little spots and stripes of a few millimetres across where a split stitch might seem clunky.

Don't worry about the edge of the satin stitch being perfect; you can cover any wobbles with the edge of the subsequent couching.

Texture variations

Kathleen Griffiths has used dappling to add texture to the serpent in her version of St Michael and the dragon. She calls him her boy-band saint; isn't he gorgeous?

He also shows great use of feathered underside couching and also the use of coloured passing threads for the background.

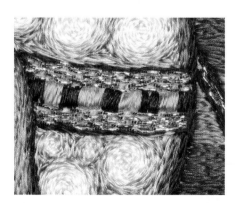

49 Finish the band by working some basic underside couching on each side of the satin stitch, by using silver passing thread to match the rest of his harness. Horse trappings are often shown in great detail in medieval art because a good horse like this would be expensive.

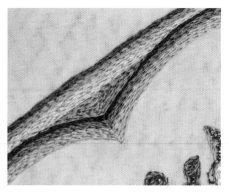

50 I am going to outline the kings' crowns with a row of split stitch before filling them with underside couching to add some more depth and to help them stand out against the background. Which colours you use is up to you, but I have chosen to mix up the colours a little for variety – so the foremost king on the blue horse has a crown outlined with ingot/gold, the rearmost king on the green horse has a crown outlined with capsicum/bright green, and the middle king on the brown horse has a crown outlined with cosmos/very dark blue. Each crown also has a couple of satin-stitched jewels matching the split stitch added on the points.

51 All three crowns are then filled with basic brick-stitch underside couching worked with very dark gold passing. Work the stitching for the crowns horizontally (that is, across the forehead), because the main area of background couching will be vertical to the image, so this will give you not only a colour contrast and a textural one but a directional contrast as well – this is something that we will explore in greater detail with the assembly of two embroidered panels into a finished purse later in the book (*see* Chapter 16).

52 I had originally left the little arcades of the framing arch blank, thinking that they would also be filled with underside couching, but, as the image has grown, I have realized that this might detract too much from the background, so I have gone back and instead just filled them in with ingot/gold, as shown, by working the stitching in a triangular fashion.

Underside-couching background patterns

I have provided the background patterns for underside couching as separate drawings for tracing, because my personal preference is to mark these background-pattern lines on after the split stitch is done. I find that the presence of a background pattern from the beginning confuses me and distracts me from the central image. However, if you prefer, you can mark it on from the very start.

I really don't recommend pencil as a transfer medium for this step, as the gold threads are quite abrasive and will rub up the graphite lines, making things look grubby – remember that, once the metallic threads are in place, you don't want to wash the piece, as these threads can tarnish if wetted.

Unless you want to draw the pattern several times, you should also avoid those fade-out pencils and pens as well. Their marks are supposed to fade after seventy-two hours, but I have found that it is often faster than that, and I don't think that I could do that much underside couching over the course of three days to justify using this medium. An hour a day for three weeks is a good allotment of time for this part: underside couching can be very hard on the hands, so little and often is preferable to trying to do it as one big binge.

I like to use the same permanent fabric-marking pen that I use for general marking out to do the backgrounds, but I try to save one that is on its last legs and thus makes a light grey line rather than a solid black one. This way, if I slip and nudge the silk stitching, there isn't enough juice in the pen to do any harm.

53 I forgive you for cursing me while transferring the background pattern for the surface couching. By the way, to warn you, it does make one's eyes go a bit wobbly too.

Take care to line up the background pattern neatly when filling in the larger areas, but there is no need to obsess over making the top area line up with the parts below – just make sure that you keep everything true to vertical.

54 Some people swear by taping the canvas to a window for transferring such patterns, but this is tricky once the fabric is laced into a frame. However, A4-sized LED light pads can be purchased quite cheaply and fit comfortably behind a typical frame for the purposes of transferring a background pattern. A lot of detail can be easily seen when using such a light source, as shown here.

55 Often, when you work an underside-couched background, you can start by working along the straight edge of the piece, but this is not the case here. Although the columns look straight, they really aren't, so, if you started by working your first row tight against the first column, the background of the whole piece will look wonky.

The best course in this case is to draw a straight line as close to the edge as you can, as shown. Use a ruler and try to line it up at right angles to the bottom of the drawing.

56 Once you get this all-important line in, you can see how wonky the columns actually are. Those of you who know your classical architecture will recall that the Parthenon is reputed to have no straight lines at all and that the slight curve fools the eye into thinking that the thing is straighter than it really is. This effect is known as entasis, and the fact that I can remember this proves that everyone who said that A-level Classics was a waste of time was very, very wrong.

Remember to use the large size 18 chenille needle for the underside couching and to wax the couching thread. For the underside couching of the background pattern, we will be using the white gold passing.

57 Work your first row of couching along this straight-edge line, couching at the points where the thread crosses the traced background lines. Remember to try to couch consistently from one side of the surface thread to the other, so that all of the surface-thread kinks lie in the same direction.

There is a limit to how small of a stitch you can make with underside couching,

because, the smaller the stitch, the more likely you are to expose the core thread below the gold, so, when it comes to the points of the diamonds of the background pattern, you have to make your own judgement as to how sharp they will be. It is a good idea to work a sample patch of this design in the margins of the piece, as it is much more difficult to execute well than anything used in the previous projects.

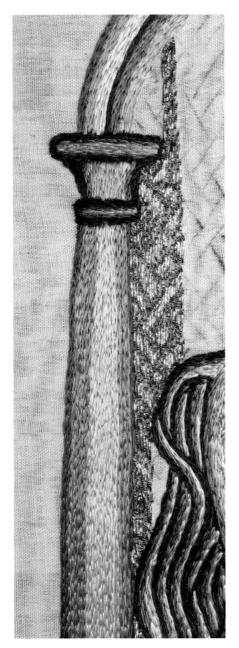

Fixing an underside-couching error

As I worked on the underside couching near the framing arch, I accidentally snagged some of the pale-blue split stitch with the point of my needle. This is an error that needs to be fixed somehow.

Pulling the snagged parts of the thread back down is well-nigh impossible, since the chances of finding the right filament to pull on at the back of the work are very slim, and unpicking the whole row could easily lead to damage to the previous rows as well. Instead, I used some of the linen thread to pull the snagged thread out of the way, as shown, to where it can soon be covered by the underside-couching gold thread.

As you can see in the accompanying image, filling in of the remaining gaps in this small area of background has covered the snag. The fact that you can't see anything of the fixed snag shows how effectively it was fixed. You to now move on to fill in the larger areas of underside couching for the rest of the background.

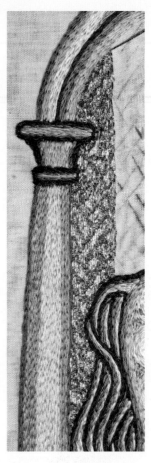

58 First, fill the background area towards the column. I have worked this whole image on its side, flipping the frame for ease of access and working from either the left or the right of the image, so, for me, working backwards is a case of getting the difficult bit over and done with, as I hate working underside couching towards my body. Working it to either side is OK, working it away from myself is the most comfortable, but working towards my body just feels plain wrong, and I always convince myself that the stitches done this way are messier and

not properly packed together. This is why it is a good idea to make a small sampler (even if it is using only the margins of your canvas to stitch doodle with) to work out how you prefer to work, because you may find it easier to work towards yourself and should plan your order of work to suit.

This advice, by the way, is very much 'do as I say, not as I do', because I am a terror for just leaping straight into things. (My way of learning seems to be mostly by messing it up and getting it right next time.)

59 As with previous projects, for the main work of the underside couching, I would always advise starting with a lower part of the composition – in this case, the areas below the horses' legs – as these areas are less noticeable when finished. This is especially relevant with this particular underside-couching pattern, as it can take a while to get your eye in, and few small mistakes below the horses' feet will not be so visible. These areas also have a shorter span for each row of passing, which makes laying down the gold thread easier.

60 Longer stretches of passing can be a bit trickier to lay flat, but you can get a better grip on the pattern. Work your way up the background until you reach the area above the kings' heads.

61 This is quite a large image, so it would be very uncomfortable to reach across to the far side when stitching. It makes sense to work half of the background from one side and then flip the frame and work the rest of the couching in the opposite direction. However, the area where the two sides meet can be tricky to get straight, so minimize it as far as possible. Don't make your meeting point the dead centre of the image! Instead, pick the narrowest point, which in this case is just above the outer point of the middle king's crown.

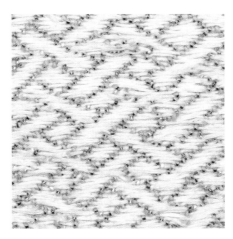

62 For reference, the underside-couching pattern should be as clear, if not clearer, on the back of the work.

63 Once all of the couching is filled in, the piece is ready to be properly mounted.

64 Red silk velvet would be the traditional choice upon which to mount this slip.

CHAPTER 12

RAPUNZEL

TECHNIQUES

Architecture, background counterpoint couching, bird, feathered wings, female face, millefleurs ground, mitred corners, trellis couching, underside-couched outlines

This and the following project in the next chapter are adapted from images on the Pienza Cope. Both are of the same size, and I have adjusted the religious imagery to be of a more secular form, so that they can be used together to make an almoner's purse, or aumoniere (*see* Chapter 16). These luxurious little purses should really be thought of as the designer handbags of the Middle Ages, and they are one of my favourite little things to make with opus anglicanum.

Rapunzel has been adapted from the image of imprisoned St Catherine on the Pienza Cope, and I have chosen this image primarily to explore the frequent use of architectural imagery in opus. I have removed two of the figures, leaving just St Catherine and Porphyry, who are now masquerading as Rapunzel and her prince.

Materials

Fabric
- Double layer of fine ramie or linen fabric (80 count), 30cm × 30cm (about 12in × 12in)

Needles
- Size 6 crewel needle
- Size 18 chenille needle
- Beading needle

Threads
- Silk-filament DeVere Yarns 6 thread, one 200m reel each, unless otherwise noted, in the following shades:
    - 19 red
       33 mid blue/turquoise
    - 38 parrot/pale blue
    - 48 crystal/white
    - 52 forget-me-not/blue
    - 55 beeswax/warm yellow
    - 60 eggshell/pale brown
    - 70 Santa/bright red
    - 73 cosmos/very dark blue
    - 74 nurse/dark blue
    - 77 honey/soft yellow
    - 105 myrtle/dark green
    - 114 basil/lime green
    - 137 cigar/very dark brown
    - 165 aran/pale brown (two reels)
    - 181 allspice/warm brown
    - 242 equator/deep red
    - 243 cactus/khaki green
    - 263 flesh

      Please note that one whole reel of each colour is more than adequate for the working of this project: any thread remaining can be used for the working of several other projects.
- Como silk thread, at least 2m (about 80in), in turquoise blue
  Please note that, if you purchase one whole 10g spool of this Como silk thread, this is more than adequate for the working of this project: any thread remaining can be used for the working of several other projects.
- Benton & Johnson smooth passing no 4, one 50m spool in very dark gold
- Benton & Johnson smooth passing no 5, 15cm (about 6in) only in silver
- Five to ten pearls of 3–4mm in diameter, or small beads of your choice (optional)

Like most of the buildings depicted in opus anglicanum, the tower here is wildly out of scale with the figures, but for me this is part of its charm.

Copes generally treat the ground underfoot in a similar fashion across the whole garment, and, for the two images that I have chosen to use from the Pienza Cope, this is also the case, but I am going to take two different approaches to achieve the same result so that we can explore different techniques for each image. Tiled floors are more popular in the later style of embroidery adopted after the plague, when the debased continental style became more popular; in contrast, most high opus anglicanum usually either has a naturalistic representation of the ground underfoot or simply ignores it completely, to leave the figures floating in mid-air.

The not-so-little birdie in the corner is there because I think that the birds tucked into the corners of the Pienza Cope are an absolute delight – and are often overlooked as mere filler– so I wanted to give them a moment in the spotlight.

Another reason for choosing images from the Pienza Cope is to explore the use of counterpoint couching. Unlike most copes, which feature homogeneous background treatments, the Pienza Cope employs different decorative backgrounds for different images, of which two are shown here, and I have also mapped out a third and provided it as an alternative. Whereas the eye-wobbling basket-weave background of The Three Kings project is created by careful placement of the underside couching, these patterns use the plainest form of underside couching, but two layers of stitching are worked in perpendicular directions to create a bolder pattern.

This design also relies heavily on the technique of leaving small gaps to be filled with underside couching, as seen previously for the St Michael Syon Cope-inspired project and The Reaper. The tower involves a much more extreme version of this technique instead of a more conventional coloured outline.

STEP-BY-STEP INSTRUCTIONS

1 Transfer the pattern on to the fabric. As with the previous project, I have left the background plain for now and will add the tracing of the background pattern once I have finished with the split stitching, but you may transfer both at once if you prefer.

2› Let's start with the tower. Using four strands of aran/pale brown, outline each brick as an individual shape, leaving a gap of about 2mm between each block. At a later stage, we will add thin rows of underside couching into these gaps, so try to keep the distance consistent. I prefer to have a fairly simple drawing to follow, so I have achieved this by working so that the pattern line is clearly visible between the bricks, but, if you wish, you can draw in your own extra lines for the mortar.

Really try to keep your mortar gaps of an even thickness, otherwise you will have problems filling them in later.

There are two ways to work the bricks so that they have crisp, defined corners: *see* the accompanying 'Mitred corners' box. The aim of both techniques is to create a visible structure within the brick that is reliant on the sheen of the silk.

Choose a direction to work in, either clockwise or anticlockwise, and try to stick with it throughout for extra consistency. In reality, you will probably find that you instinctively work one way or the other, depending on which is your dominant hand.

Method one: outer edge first

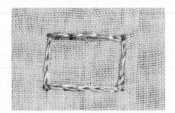

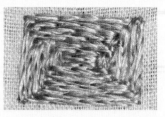

1 The most obvious way to create a crisp mitred corner for the bricks is to work from the outside in towards the centre, starting by working an outline. This allows for very precise placement of the brick as a whole.

2 I have worked my samples by using contrasting colours to show how the second row of stitching should bite out slightly into the first row at each corner. Without this, it would be all too easy for the interior to become a round-edged spiral, and for gaps to subsequently appear in the corners of the brick. This is really just an extension of the general principle of always splitting something.

3 This action of biting out into the corners creates an affect not unlike that of the popular log-cabin blocks made by quilters.

4 This overlapping is continued until the central area is easily covered by a row or two of stitching.

Method two: working out from the centre

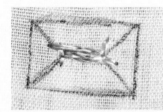

3 The next layer of stitching covers up the extended arms of the previous stitching layer, and so on. Throwing each corner out into an exaggerated spike again prevents the corners from becoming rounded by lazy stitching. (I am not accusing, I am just as guilty of idleness as anyone else: it is simply human nature to try to cut corners – literally, in this case.) Giving the final edge neat corners covers up the spikes of the previous row.

1 In this case, I have marked the canvas with a sort of envelope shape to help judge where to begin. Basically, each end of the central row of stitching should be equidistant from the two nearest corners. You can mark this line carefully by first measuring if you find that easier, but normally I just guesstimate its length and placement.

2 The next row is worked around this central line, but with the corners overextended like the arms of a windmill.

As you can clearly see from my sample, even if you carefully measure your starting point, it can still be necessary to add extra bulk to one side of your brick shape to achieve the desired dimensions; in this case, I had to add an extra row of cream on the right-hand side.

There are pros and cons to each method, and the sensible thing is to use both methods depending on what kind of rectangle, square or other polygon you are trying to make. I find that working out from the central line gives much sharper corners and a better overall fill but works better for very regular shapes. Working in from the edge is far more sensible for irregular shapes such as the curved bricks on the left-hand tower, where measuring a central starting point is more difficult. I suggest that you try to stitch a small brick by using each method, to allow you to practise before beginning work on the tower.

3 It is hard to see the effect of this crisp mitring approach when the piece is viewed flat on, and is even harder to photograph flat, so this picture was taken at an angle, hence the slight distortion.

For contrast and for reference, the left-hand tower has been worked with each brick being stitched from the centre out, and the right-hand tower with each brick being stitched from the edge inwards. There isn't a huge difference between the two results, so use which method you find easiest to work.

The importance of shine

You can clearly see here the subtle effect given by careful stitching with the silk; there is a clear difference between the areas filled as flat shapes, such as at the very top of each turret, and the bricks. Once the piece is taken off of the frame and allowed to move, it will fully come alive.

It might be ever so slightly mind-numbing to work so many repeated elements, but the finished result is more than worth it. This use of silk to create shine and dimension is just as much an important part of opus anglicanum as the shine of the gold, and this is where silk filament comes into its own – you will never get the same effect with a more mundane thread.

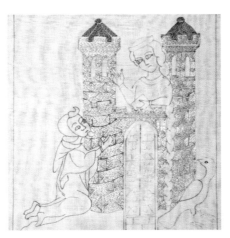

4 Use forget-me-not/blue for stitching the tower roof, again leaving tiny gaps for underside couching later on. I have worked the triangles by going back up to the top of the shape each time, so that all of the stitches flow down the roof, but working around each shape in a spiral is an equally valid choice.

6 Myrtle/dark green is used for working the door and, again, remember to leave narrow gaps for later couching. You are not trying to add texture here: the green is merely a foil for the underside couching to be added later, but the curls of ironwork on the door are much trickier to get right than the straight geometric mortar between bricks, so be careful with your spacing.

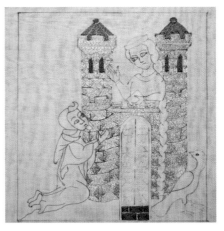

5 Use allspice/warm brown to fill in the upper-tower openings and the doorstep bricks.

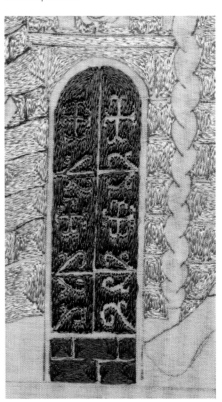

7 Again, I have worked all of my stitches in the same direction, which, with this particular green, creates an almost oily sheen. Pack the stitches with extra care to avoid leaving gaps. My usual admonition to always split something doesn't apply where the green stops for the ironwork, but be careful to fill out to the end of each row of stitching with a half stitch, rather than leaving a narrow end to the row.

8 The ground is worked with alternating rows of cactus/khaki green and basil/lime green, with each colour row being of four or five rows of stitching.

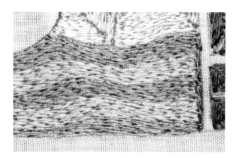

9 I have added a bit of wiggle by partly layering some of the rows, to make the width inconsistent, and I have worked down from the top, but it is just as valid to work upwards in poker-straight rows starting from the bottom edge.

This treatment is fine as it is, and you can leave it like that if you want to, but I am going to add flowers.

Tip

Don't worry about getting it 'right': there is no right, and the flowers are no more complicated than the ones that a child would draw with a crayon, and, if you can draw it with a crayon, you can sew it without a pattern. Plus, these are tiny flowers, each less than a couple of centimetres high — you would have to work pretty hard to screw it up!

11 Next, add some petals at the top of the stem and a couple of buds — literally two stitches — at the ends of the side branches. It doesn't have to look botanically perfect: it is just a cartoon representation of a flower, and it does not matter if yours ends up being a bit abstract — the viewer's brain will know that it is a flower.

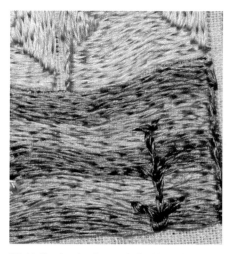

10 Unlike for the Rumpelstiltskin project (*see* Chapter 13), where big bold flowers are sewn first and the ground is shaped around them, for this panel, we are going to do things the other way around, which is why the flowers aren't part of the pattern drawing.

We are aiming for a late-medieval millefleurs pattern, like the one seen on the famous Lady and the Unicorn tapestries from Paris, so we are just going to scatter some foliage around at random.

Just draw a stem, that is, a straight line worked with four strands of myrtle/dark green. Make sure there is still room for the petals, and splay out two stitches at the top of the stem, to give the petals somewhere to sit. Then add two tiny leaves — of no more than three or four stitches — for the petals at the base. Be sure to split the ends of the leaves into each other to create a point. Add two extra stems branching out of the stem about halfway up it.

That is all you need to do: it is little more than a doodle. Practise at the edge before committing to the main canvas if you need to.

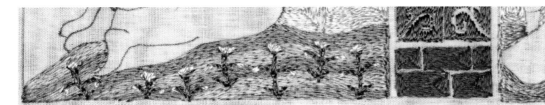

12 Scatter little flowers all over the green stuff. A good medieval term for this type of pattern is powdered. Just enjoy sewing the pretty little daisies, and don't sweat about making them perfect or spacing them an even distance apart: nature doesn't bother, so why would you?

13 Outline Rapunzel's dress with equator/deep red. Where she is hiding behind the balcony, add some depth to this clothing by working deep triangles of stitching, to add shade.

14 Use Santa/bright red for adding a second layer of colour. Reds are much more difficult to shade than blues and greens, as the highlight tone can often be either too pink or too harsh. In this case, the highlight is quite a tinny red, so I want to minimize it by using the two darker tones more heavily.

15 Lastly, add stitching with red, for the highlight.

16› Tiny areas of trellis couching are often used to add texture and detail to opus anglicanum, so use some here for rendering the cover of the book that Rapunzel is holding. Use forget-me-not/blue for the laid background with a single strand of gold for the trellis, couched at the points of intersection with the same blue. Use a very short strand of gold to avoid it shredding, and give the needle a good wiggle while working the trellis to make a big enough hole for the thread to pass through without damage. Gold thread is very prone to twisting at the back of the canvas when used in this way, so try to run it around your finger as you pull it through, to prevent this from happening.

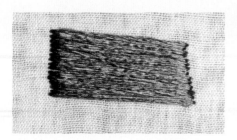

1 Use six or eight strands of filament at once, as the first layer of thread should be quite thick, to achieve good coverage of the canvas. Simply go back and forth to cover the area, but this isn't satin stitch: bring the needle straight back up immediately next to where you took it down, travelling across no more than a single thread of the background canvas, leaving barely any thread at the back.

Every now and then, you will pop the thread straight back out again, this is annoying, but it means that you are approaching this right. Really pack the rows of thread together, because you don't want the couching thread to later push them apart, and, the better packed they are, the less likely this is to happen.

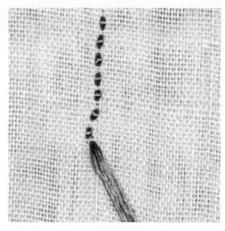

2 Once the area is filled, all that should be visible at the back of the work is a row of tiny stab stitches on each side of the filled area, plus any ends from where you needed to anchor the thread at the beginning and end of the stitching.

If, when you turn the work over, you notice that you have looped the thread around once or twice, don't beat yourself up and think you have to unpick – just try not to do it again. Remember that silk thread was eye-wateringly expensive in the Middle Ages, and be as parsimonious regarding your thread as a Yorkshireman would be – keep it all at the front where you can show it off.

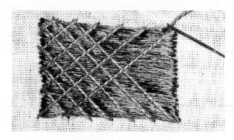

3 Obviously, that huge wedge of shiny silk will be completely unstable once you take your embroidery off the frame – it would catch and be ruined in minutes – so the next step is to stabilize it, which we are going to do very prettily.

Take a contrasting colour, or perhaps a strand of metal thread (you can even use a spun or plied thread for this stage), and lay it over the top of the silk at an angle of roughly 45 degrees; do this by bringing the threaded needle up on one side of the filled area and down on the opposite side, much as you did when creating the filled area. If you are working a large area of trellis couching, you may find that the silk wanders around a bit, and you will therefore have to periodically nudge it back into line with the couching thread.

Continue to lay down couching threads at this angle in one direction, then lay another layer over that one at right angles, to create a trellis.

Again, you shouldn't be passing this couching thread over the back of the work; you should be working around the edge of the shape to waste as little thread as possible.

Tips

Getting the couching-thread angle consistent is vital for a neat result. The best way to achieve this is to hold the thread in place and adjust the angle before putting the needle down through the fabric. This is especially true for the first row, and, if you get that nice and neat, you can use it as a guide for the placement of the rest of the top layer.

The couching threads will also wander a bit, but with practice you will be able to nudge them back into line at the final stage.

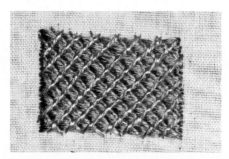

4 The whole thing is still unstable, so take another thread and place a small stab stitch over each intersection of the trellis. This can be of the same colour as is the trellis, or you can use a third colour, as I have done here.

I prefer to use a single stab stitch, but you can use a small cross too. A single stitch is more unobtrusive; a cross is better if you want to emphasize a colour contrast.

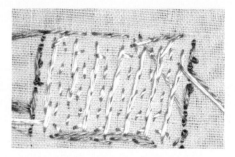

5 Once again, there should be very little stitching for the couching threads showing at the back of the work.

17 Outline her face and hands with four strands of cigar/very dark brown, and stitch a double row at the brows.

Fill in her eyes with crystal/white and whatever colour you fancy (I used forget-me-not/blue, but you could give her hazel or green eyes, if you prefer).

Because she is a princess, and all princesses are contractually obliged to have lips as red as roses, we are going to stray from the normal opus anglicanum straight-line mouth and give her a splash of red lipstick. I have used Santa/bright red, but you could give her a more sultry lip with the darker red, or a spot of pink would give a more innocent look.

Uses of trellis couching

By the way, if you are ever embroidering a stylish fourteenth-century lady, this is the perfect technique to apply for stitching her fashionable hairnet.

Trellis couching was also often used to add texture to cushions and pillows in original pieces of opus.

18 For her flesh, go down from using four strands of thread to two. I have veered away from the usual sallow flesh colours of opus and used flesh, which is a bit more of a natural flesh tone.

Her hands are simply straight lines of stitching radiating out from the wrist, but remember to split out of and into the outline wherever necessary.

20 Her forehead should be similarly smooth and unfurrowed. Connect it to one cheek by working the first few rows split out of the cheek and going straight across to the other side of her brow. When working the last row, continue the stitching line over one brow and down the profile of the nose to connect back to the cheek. Work all of the rows in the same direction, to keep her skin smooth, and remember to always split out of or into something if at all possible.

19 Keep her looking young and beautiful by giving her nice high cheekbones. First, to define a tendon of her neck, add a thin, gently curved line of stitching running from her neck, as shown, to connect to the apple and continue by stitching this apple from the outside spiralling inwards. Work the apples of her cheeks as perfect circles (or at least as near perfect as you can manage), making sure to hit the lower edge of the eyes and the edge of her nose.

Tip

I find that it helps to picture the classic image of Princess Diana with her head demurely tilted while I work on female opus faces, as it is a very similar look that we are after — it is a way of meditating upon the intended outcome.

21 Every face is slightly different, even when worked to a formula as for many opus faces. In this case, I have started working her nose as part of the underbrow, which is itself split out from the line worked up the side of the face, creating a smooth flow of skin. If you run your finger starting from the side of your face just above the ear, there is a natural path below your brow line that connects to the side of your nose – all you have to do is echo that with your needle.

22 Fill in the remaining areas of her face, using the triangular stitching for filling any tiny gaps between the larger areas. Work her chin out of the side of the cheek and curl around the mouth, remembering to maintain a consistent direction of stitching.

23 Accentuate the tilt of her head by filling in her neck on the diagonal, in keeping with the gently curved line of stitching added when working the cheeks.

24 Her hair is up next. Unlike the normal way of stitching hair in opus, where you can have a little bit of fun, stitching a plait is more like stitching a piece of Celtic knotwork, because you have to take a more systematic approach.

Because her hair is a very pale golden blonde, there is a danger that it will melt into the background against the cream-coloured tower; therefore, start by adding some lowlights with allspice/warm brown. A single-row outline is all that is needed, but let it kick into the body of the plait, to represent the shadows where the hair interlaces and to add some dimension.

25 Work her hair by alternating the stitching of one row of beeswax/warm yellow with two rows of honey/soft yellow. Start by working the hair around the top of her head in the normal way, using one needle for each colour, then, as you work down the braid, you need to braid the stitching just as you would plait a little girl's hair. Work the first chunk of hair as a block that finishes slightly under where the next section will go, then work that section so that it covers the messy ends of the previous one.

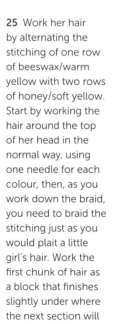

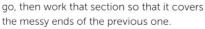

26 As you can see here, this approach gives the hair a subtle braided effect.

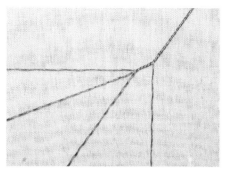

28 Take a strand of the thick, blue Como silk, untwist it a little to release the four separate strands, and pull out one of these strands and use it for the split-stitch filling of the bluebird's body.

27 Rapunzel is a princess, so obviously all of the cute little woodland creatures are her besties, especially the bluebird of happiness. He needs to be started with a touch of red, though, to visually tie him to his princess pal, because, if she is the only splash of red in the composition, she will overpower everything else and make the image top heavy. So, outline his body with equator/deep red and his beak and legs with Santa/bright red, as well as giving him a touch of red eyeliner and some crystal/white stitching for his eye.

29 Our bird is filled as several blocks of blue Como silk stitching, with no shading other than that resulting from the shapes of the stitching, so work his body and neck as a circuit of stitches that curl around his eye. His leg is worked as a separate shape to add definition, and then the top of his tail is worked with all of the stitching going in the same direction, to lead into his feathers.

Next, fill the bar across his wing with Santa/bright red and the top of the wing and feathers with alternating blocks of cosmos/very dark blue and parrot/pale blue.

30 Use a whole strand of the blue Como silk to depict the feathers of his tail with feathered underside couching before adding spines worked with equator/deep red.

31› Next, the prince's robe is outlined in cosmos/very dark blue. Notice how the folds of the robe outline the shape of the body and limbs below; use two or three rows of silk to emphasize the deeper folds of the cloth, but don't outline the edges that will eventually have fur trim. His coif should also be outlined with this blue.

32 Forget-me-not/blue is used for adding the second layer of colour. Be a little bit more heavy handed with this colour, to make it the dominant shade and to help emphasize the folds. Notice that some of the folds that lie in shadow haven't got room left for the highlight colour and so add depth to the image.

Note also that a thin channel is deliberately left at the sleeves and hem of the robe.

A note about white

Having bright-white linens was not only a mark of wealth, showing that the wearer could afford enough changes of clothes to be constantly clean, but also a mark of the good virtue of the wife of the household in keeping all spick and span – modern laundry-related advertising's obsession with whites that are whiter than white has very ancient roots.

33 The remaining areas of the robe are filled with parrot/pale blue. Remember to always split out of and into the stitching of the previous colour (especially in the tight curves and corners) and to use a unified stitching direction.

35 Use crystal/white to fill in the rest of the fur. The prince's white coif is filled as a flat shape with the stitches curling into a spiral from the outer edge. If you decide to add some shading to the white coif, take care – more than one or two rows of a shading colour at the edge will dominate the white, and the coif will then read as that colour rather than as white.

Again, if you decide to add shading to white, bear in mind that the colour that you shade with should be very pale, and it will also influence the perceived shade of the white. Pale-grey shading will easily look grubby, pale blue will look clean, and cream or yellow will generally look old or stained.

34 Add the texture of fur to the lining of the robe with allspice/warm brown. This is similar to the fur on the robes of The Three Kings project, but it is a hint of luxurious lining here rather than big panels of it, so it becomes just a series of triangles along the edge; however, it still adds a sense of movement to the garment.

36 Use four strands of cigar/very dark brown to outline his face, hands and shoes. Fill in the pupils and whites of the eyes.

The prince doesn't get ruby-red lips: he just gets the usual slightly disapproving line of a mouth – perhaps he is worried that his robe is getting dirty in the mud?

37 Equator/deep red is used for filling in the shoes, but here it looks more brown next to the dark-brown outline; however, using a tiny bit of red on the prince, as well as on the bird, emphasizes the visual triangle created by the relationship between the three figures of the composition.

A smidge of Santa/bright red is also used to fill the channels along the edges of the robe. You could use gold, as is often done on the robes of opus figures, but I like this hint of red.

38 As for the princess, his hands are simply packed tightly with lines of stitching radiating out from the wrists. I have used two strands of eggshell/pale brown for working the prince's skin, which is a far more traditional opus skin tone.

39 Again as for the princess, his cheeks are high and firm. His face is much smaller than hers, and it can be quite challenging to add character to smaller faces, so pay attention to each stitch and proceed with care – Rapunzel won't want to marry him if he ends up looking like a Hapsburg.

40 The side of his face is quite visible, so tie the cheeks to the forehead by working out of the apple of the cheek before going up and across the forehead and then down the nose. This creates an arch to his brow and makes him look imploring.

The rest of the forehead should be worked across the face from left to right. Remember to pack the rows as closely together as you can, and use the outline to split out of and into.

41 The underbrow can then be worked by splitting out of the cheek and arching the stitching around, as shown.

42 His chin is mostly obscured by his beard, so it is just a case of working across under and over his lips, remembering to split out of and into the previously made stitches, and maintaining a uniform direction of stitching.

43 Now, his neck can be filled in, still by using the eggshell/pale brown thread.

44 Obviously, your prince can have any colour of hair that pleases you, but I have given him hair worked in alternating double rows of allspice/warm brown and beeswax/ warm yellow. You can put some curls into his quiff and his hair, but his beard is just a series of small tufts, to create a silly little beard.

45› One of the really tricky jobs for this project is working the pointing on the tower, and the details on the tower roof, by adding underside-couched very dark gold.

Most of the mortar should be as wide as two or three rows of underside couching and be worked in the basic basket-weave pattern. It is fiddly to work and involves a lot of plunging of loose ends, but it is not actually any more difficult than filling a large area.

One snag that will crop up more often is that you will find that the needle will pull

quite a few ends of silk through from the back, but 99 per cent of these ends will be pulled back down again on the return pass of the couching thread.

The ironwork of the door is worked with the same narrow strips of inserted underside couching as the mortar, but in this case you need to work gentle curves into the couching. Do the mortar first, so that you can get into the swing of things, then tackle the slightly trickier door.

46 One thing that I have left until last is the collar of Rapunzel's dress, because I wasn't sure whether I wanted to do it with gold or a colour. Sometimes, you just need to set something aside and come back to it. Gold would look fine here, but I felt like I wanted to pull some more blue up from the base of the composition, so I have used some of the blue Como silk thread again and underside couched that into her collar and cuffs.

47 As I previously mentioned, you can draw in the background pattern at the same time as you draw the main image, but I prefer to do it when I get there. In this case, I am really glad that I didn't have the background drawn in when I was working on the rest, because this pattern makes my eyes go a bit wobbly.

One thing that you notice over and over again with historical textiles is how modern some of the patterns can be. This one is based on quite rigid geometry, and I am sure that, if you looked, you would find examples of it from other periods of history as well – and I bet you that they would all make my eyes go just as wobbly.

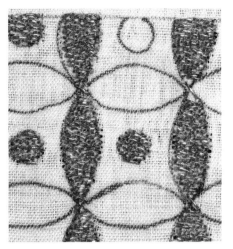

48 The background pattern is created by counterpoint couching, so we are going to work one area of the pattern first, using a vertical basket-weave pattern, and then fill in the rest by using the same basket-weave pattern worked on the horizontal axis. The play of light between the two different directions is what will create the contrast of the design; as with every aspect of opus, what you are really manipulating is light. You can use two slightly different shades of gold thread to add to this effect, but I am using just the one, as the result is far more subtle. The danger of using two shades is that the background can come to dominate the whole image, especially here, where there is quite a lot going on with the architecture already.

In the smaller areas of the pattern, you just have to sort of muddle through, but, with the large area on the left, the most efficient approach is to work a row of marquise shapes almost like a string of beads. Notice that, where four marquise shapes overlap, I have skipped over the join with a diagonal stitch made on the surface. I have also added the central dots as I went along, but you can do them all on one go, if you prefer.

The most important thing to remember here is to keep all of your rows of couching on the same axis. You could draw some extra lines on the background as a guide if you wanted to, but this pattern is made of small repeated elements and, if you line up your drawing with the weave of the canvas, it shouldn't be difficult to stay roughly on track. This is a good starter pattern for this technique – the one that I use for the Rumpelstiltskin project (*see* Chapter 13) is considerably more challenging.

Smooth-passing alternatives

I have listed Benton & Johnson smooth passing as the gold thread for this project, but I am actually using some vintage stuff that I picked up for a song on eBay (the listed very dark gold passing no 4 is almost identical but a good bit tougher: with the modern passing, you can 'pass' it through the canvas, that is, sew a stitch or two with it at a pinch, but my vintage stuff is too delicate for that).

My vintage thread is softer than the modern stuff and shreds more easily; you can see that more of the core thread shows than with the Benton & Johnson passing threads that I have used for the other projects. Nevertheless, I like it because it tarnishes a little bit over time and adds an interesting depth of colour. Every brand of gold thread behaves slightly differently to the next, so you need to adapt your technique to your materials.

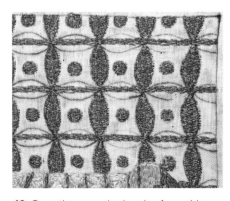

49 Once the marquise beads of couching are worked in one direction, you can work long bars of couching right over the intersections. By maximizing the length of the rows, you minimize the amount of finishing work, as you have less faffing about to do for plunging the ends.

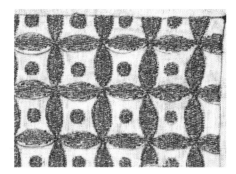

50 Once you have the interconnecting bars in place, work on each side of them to round out the bead shapes.

Counterpoint couching

Counterpoint couching just means stitching the same brick-stitch underside couching but at a 90-degree angle to the rest of the pattern, that is, part of the underside-couching pattern is worked with the stitches all running in one direction and the rest of the pattern is worked with the stitches all running in the perpendicular direction. It sounds simple, and it is, but great care must be taken not to break any of the metal threads of the existing stitching.

Often, it can be tricky to find a place to get the needle through the canvas at this stage, so it is important to do as little plunging of ends as possible and to try to work with the longest single run of underside-couching stitches that you can.

51 Now that the main structure of the pattern is in place, it is time to fill in the background areas with the counterpoint stitching. The background pattern is a touch too dominant at the moment, and filling in the background will adjust the balance of the composition.

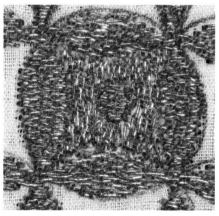

53 The next stage involves fiddling around filling the two final corners and the last side. I am not going to lie to you: the corners are hard to do, and you will get thoroughly sick of them. The best thing to do with multiple-repeat patterns such as this is to tell yourself that you are going to do two or three a day, because breaking it down into achievable small units will stop you from going crackers or just giving up out of sheer repetitive boredom (unless you are one of those people who thrives on repetition, in which case, you will be in your element).

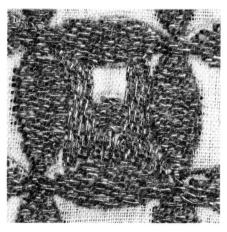

52 Start working the counterpoint couching in one corner. It doesn't really matter which, but in this instance I started at the bottom right by plunging the initial thread right down into the tiny gap between the edges of the circles and working out from there until my rows were going straight up and down. You have to work around the central dot, remembering that the rows must stay strictly at right angles to the first set of stitches, so you can't bend around the dot. As a child, I was always the messy kid who coloured outside the lines; now, you have to colour very neatly within them, back and forth.

Go up and down to one side of the dot – it doesn't matter which, just whichever side you happen to find yourself at once the long row nudges the dot. Once you get to the other side, fill the rest of the space with long rows until you eventually work into one of the corners (again, it doesn't matter which).

By carefully working up and down, you can fill all but one side of the dot and two corners in one swoop.

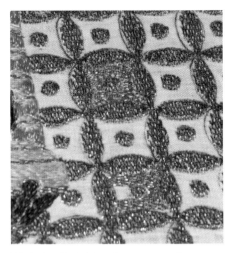

54 As for the bricks, these repeat elements worked with counterpoint couching can seem a bit dead when viewed flat, but they come to life when viewed from an angle, as shown.

55 Once you have finally filled in around all of the circles, you are nearly there. We just need a couple of minor touches to finish up.

56 Use a single strand of crystal/white silk thread to surface couch a double strand of silver passing around the edges of our princess's circlet, being sure to leave a gap down the centre. If you have very small pearls, you might want to add three or four layers of silver first, so that the canvas won't show through once you couch on the pearls. Overall, the gap that you leave depends on the size of your pearls: it should be just a smidge smaller than the full width of the pearl, so that the pearl sits snugly between the lines of metal. Real pearls are natural and full of variations, so no two batches will be identical, but man-made glass beads should be more consistently sized – work with what you have and are comfortable with using.

57 Add the pearls, being careful not to overcrowd them. If you don't have – or don't want to use – pearls, you could add a stripe of satin stitch worked with alternating colours, as I did for The Three Kings project for the blue horse's breast band. Remember to put the satin stitch in first, before the couching goes over the top, to get a neat result. Using alternating colours is not only a medieval practice, but it also creates the illusion of beads. (I am fairly certain that this was the intention in many cases.)

58 Now you are ready to mount the project, either as a framed piece or as a panel as part of a purse (*see* Chapter 16).

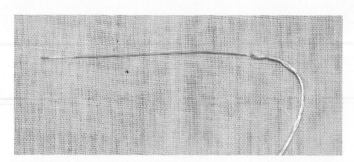

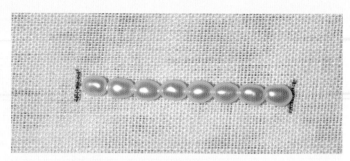

1 It is fine to use fake pearls, but try to avoid the plastic ones and go for glass, as it has a better lustre. Fake pearls are actually authentic, as evidenced by the frequent issuing of sumptuary laws banning their use – you don't repeatedly tell people not to do something if they are not doing it in the first place. Nothing beats the subtle, expensive lustre of a real pearl, though, and freshwater or cultivated ones aren't much more expensive than a decent fake.

The one downside to using real pearls is that they tend to have ridiculously small holes, so you need a special needle. Standard beading needles often won't fit through pearls (in fact, I have some 1mm-diameter pearls that are so tiny that I have to use them on the string that they came threaded on, discarding any that are surplus to requirements); instead, you will need the superfine ones.

The needles that I typically use are made by Milward, who make the finest beading needles that I have found; you want a packet of needles of sizes 10–13 to go through the holes made in natural pearls. These needles are stupidly fine and very bendy. They are also a nightmare to thread, so don't say that I didn't warn you. In fact, my photographer took one look at this needle and asked if it really is a needle.

2 There is a right way and a wrong way to attach pearls.

The wrong way is to carefully measure the space to be filled and then fill it with pearls and anchor both ends, as seen here.

Note the black marks on the canvas that delineate the beginning and end of the row. At this stage, the pearls sit comfortably between the marks, but...

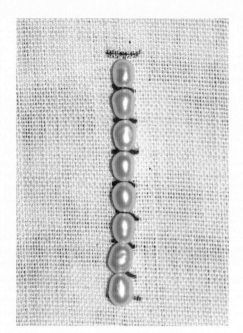 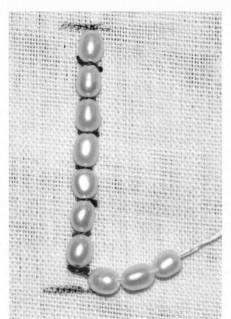 

3 ...once both ends of the thread are anchored, if you then place a couching stitch between each pearl (I have used blue thread here so that you can see it; normally, you would use white to blend in), the couching stitch, even though the silk is very fine, pushes the pearls apart slightly. If you compare this with the first picture, you can clearly see that the couching stitches have pushed the row of pearls over the black mark by about half a pearl. The longer your row of pearls, the more the couching stitches will push them apart, so that, if you carefully measure and then anchor a long row of, say, twenty or thirty pearls, by the time you have sewn the majority of them down, there won't be enough space for the rest of them. Stubbornly trying to force extra pearls into a small space can often lead to unsightly buckling.

4 It is far better to thread the pearls and then leave the needle end unanchored. When you get to the end of the space that you want to fill, having worked the couching stitches one by one from the other, anchored, end of the line of pearls, you can simply remove any excess pearls and save them for next time.

5 Once you have removed the excess pearls from the thread, then you can anchor it. It looks far better to have the pearls fall a millimetre or two short than it does to overcrowd them.

CHAPTER 13

RUMPELSTILTSKIN

TECHNIQUES

Background counterpoint couching, falcons, female face, flowers, ground, peacock, peacock feathers, sheep, surface couching of details

As for the previous project, this one adapts a religious image from the Pienza Cope to a secular story. Here, St Margaret encountering the provost Olybrius are substituted for the miller's poor daughter minding her own business while her idiot father is off boasting to the king about her prowess as a spinner.

One of the things that fascinates me about fairy tales is all the different versions around the world, from the ancient Egyptian version of Cinderella, to the medieval Italian version of Sleeping Beauty (which to me is basically an early date-rape tale, where the princess is awoken by labour pains nine months after the prince's 'kiss'), to versions told by twenty-first-century science fiction writers. Fairy tales are universal and often much grimmer than the modern Disney versions would have us believe.

Materials

- Double layer of fine ramie or linen fabric (80 count), 30cm x 30cm (about 12in x 12in)

Needles
- Size 8 crewel needle
- Size 18 chenille needle
- Beading needle

Threads
- Silk-filament DeVere Yarns 6 thread, one 200m reel each in the following shades:
  - 13 brown/light brown
  - 28 violet/bright purple
  - 44 black ebony
  - 50 lily/white
  - 53 foil/silver grey
  - 71 cappuccino/pale brown
  - 73 cosmos/very dark blue
  - 104 avocado/very dark green
  - 108 capsicum/bright green
  - 127 tinge/very pale grey
  - 137 cigar/very dark brown
  - 152 robin/bright red
  - 167 clementine/orange
  - 181 allspice/warm brown
  - 211 blush/strawberry pink
  - 242 equator/deep red
  - 255 chilli/dark red
  - 313 paradise blue/dark turquoise
  - 321 ivy/mid green
    Please note that one whole reel of each colour is more than adequate for the working of this project: any thread remaining can be used for the working of several other projects.
- Benton & Johnson smooth passing no 4, one 50m spool in very dark gold
- Benton & Johnson smooth passing no 5, one 50m spool in white gold
- Benton & Johnson smooth passing no 6, at least 50cm (about 20in) in silver
- Benton & Johnson twist, only 15cm (about 6in), in dark gold
  Please note that one 50m spool of a single colour of no 4 or no 5 smooth passing will suffice if you choose to work the counterpoint couching in monochrome, rather than with the two different shades that I have used here for added contrast.
- Strong linen thread, for couching
- Lacing thread

Additional materials
- Beeswax, for waxing linen thread
- Three pearls of 3–4mm in diameter (suggested size) or small beads of your choice (optional)

Here, we will be using twist for the first time, for working the peacock's crown. Twist is simply two strands of standard smooth passing twisted around one another, hence the name. It gives a more substantial thread, but we will need only fifteen centimetres (about six inches) of it. If you don't want to go to the expense of buying a whole reel of twist, you could just take thirty centimetres (about twelve inches) or so of standard smooth passing of your chosen thickness and twist it around upon itself to make a loose twist – anyone who spins will be familiar with the procedure of plying two threads, and there are plenty of how-to videos on YouTube to help.

STEP-BY-STEP INSTRUCTIONS

So, after discovering that there is an Arabic version of Rumpelstiltskin, I decided to feature a Persian miller's daughter, because I have been wanting to do an opus face in a non-traditional opus skin tone for quite some time. In the end, I made her far darker than a Persian princess ought to be, because the shade that I chose to use looks gorgeous with her bright-orange robe, and I am a sucker for a good colour combination. If you choose to give her a more properly Persian coffee-coloured skin, or even a traditional opus anglicanum so-pasty-that-she-might-actually-be-dead skin tone, my advice is that it might be a good idea to pick out a more subtle set of shades for her robes.

The suspicious-minded amongst you might suspect that I have bumped off poor old Olybrius because his name is too hard to spell, but few things are harder to spell than is Rumpelstiltskin.

Which is why I also left Rumpelstiltskin out and replaced him with a glorious peacock! The spellcheck doesn't complain about peacocks. Peacocks are also a symbol of royalty in Persian folklore, so he can be read as a precursor to the miller's daughter's promotion to queen at the end of the story.

In addition to which, the peacock lurking in the margins of the Pienza Cope is one of my favourite bits of opus anglicanum. To add to the animal theme of this project, we also have some ovine companions here. As you can see in the corner, there is a nice and normal white sheep (like everyone else's families), plus, a gormless, cross-eyed black sheep – how could anyone possibly resist that deranged little face? That little black sheep is like a medieval image of every single member of my family: I couldn't possibly have ignored him.

This project also includes an even more complicated pattern to work with counterpoint couching, to continue our birdie theme for the almoner's purse or aumoniere that we will assemble in Chapter 16.

1 Transfer the pattern on to the fabric.

As with the previous projects, I have left the background plain for now and will add the tracing of the background pattern once I have finished split stitching, but you may transfer both at once if you prefer.

2 Begin by laying down the contour lines of the ground with avocado/very dark green, using two rows of stitching throughout. Split out from this baseline to grow the flower stems, also with double lines; don't worry if the stems look a little chunky, as they will slim down when they are crowded in by the background stitches.

3 Use a single row of blush/strawberry pink to outline the shapes of the flower petals, adding an extra petal by stitching across the centre of each flower.

4 Next, fill each flower with lily/white, being careful to pack the stitches closely together. Split into the pink outline to blend the two colours a little. The petals are very tiny, so only a few stitches are needed to fill each one.

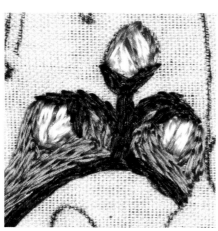

5 Now begin to fill the ground with ivy/mid green. The aim is to work in one continuous direction across the width of the image, but, of course, the flower stems are in the way, and we have to work around them, which is part of how we add contouring to the landscape. So, start by hugging the dark-green line and follow it up the flower stem until you have to tuck the stitching under the flowers, then continue adding layers by working along the same stitching route until the area under the flowers is completely full.

6 When the next row starts to bump into the tip of a flower, flare up the rows of stitching by using layering and perhaps a triangular stitch as needed until the green reaches to the top edge of the first flower, as shown. The aim is to make the mid-green stitches form a mound over the top of each clump of flowers and make the ground look undulating, so adding some layered stitches helps to achieve this.

7 You should now have created a slope of stitches that will allow you to work up and over the lower flower and fill in the area beneath the top stem, at which point you can repeat the layering process so that the green is flush with the tip of the top flower.

There is never any shame in realizing that you have left a tiny gap and going back to fill it with a stitch or two. Often, you won't even realize that the gap is there until you take the embroidery off of the frame and get some movement into the fabric. Looking at a massively blown-up image of this tiny flower, I can see a couple of spots where I need to go back and add a stitch or two – nobody is perfect.

8 Once the flowers are incorporated into their little green mounds, you can work over the top of them to contour the landscape. You may want to add extra layering to the green bits to help to add shape, but I would suggest at least three rows of stitching over the top of each flower.

I haven't marked out where the different areas of green should go beyond the first dark contour line, because there is no real right or wrong to it – work as much of this green as looks good to you.

Make sure that the result is nice and wiggly, though. Wiggly is good for ground.

9 Now we can go on to fill the remainder of the landscape with capsicum/bright green. You need to make sure that you get enough green under the peacock's feet and under our girl's bum so that the landscape is supporting its inhabitants, but, other than that, the top line of the ground on my drawing is simply a guide – you can make the top edge as jagged or a wiggly as you like.

You will need to use some layering and flaring out to get a smooth finish, so remember to always split something.

10 The two sheep are up next. They are quite small compared to the human figure if you are used to modern sheep, but most ancient breeds are tiny compared to modern animals – look up the Boreray breed to see what I mean: cute and tiny.

Outline both sheep with four strands of cappuccino/pale brown. Give the foremost sheep some curly locks of hair, but the black sheep should have stripes to denote longer wool.

Fill in their eyes in the usual way with a spot of black and white, and you may as well use a spot of the same pink as used for the flowers for the black sheep's silly little tongue. Make sure that you give him crossed eyes, so that he looks especially silly.

12› Fill the bodies and horns of both sheep by using four strands of thread – lily/white for the front sheep and cigar/very dark brown for the sheep at the back. As with the grass, you will need to use layering to fill the shapes.

Filling white stitching over a white fabric is much more forgiving than filling a dark colour over a white canvas, and, having a good look at this photo enlarged, I can now see a few gaps. Again, with this technique, there is no shame in going back and filling the odd gap later; it is really easy to miss a bit, and it is better to notice it now and fix it than realize that it is there once a piece is finished.

11 Elaborate the white sheep's locks with a touch of foil/silver grey, and also fill in her horns and hooves. Use the same colour to emphasize the black sheep's woolly stripes, but leave her horns to be filled in later.

13 Go down to using two strands of thread to fill their faces. Not only would four threads look clunky here but real sheep have much finer, shorter hair on their faces than the rest of their bodies. I suppose that they wouldn't be able to see otherwise.

14 Use a single row of equator/deep red to outline the miller's daughter's robe. You really don't need more than a single row here, as it is just going to add some depth.

While you have this colour of thread in your needle, use a little bit of it to colour in the whorl of the spindle held in her right hand: work the whorl as a solid block of colour.

15 Reinforce the dark lines of the robe with a touch of chilli/dark red. Again, I have used a very light touch with this colour, of never more than two lines of stitching deep, because I want to make the lovely bright orange very dominant in her robe.

‹**16** A little bit of robin/bright red is added next, and, in places, I have allowed the use of three rows of this shade, to round out the curves and folds of her robe.

All of these rows of colour have been built up by using a consistent stitching direction and remembering to always split out of and into the previous stitches.

17 Finally, remembering to keep the consistent stitching direction, fill in all of the blank areas of her robe with the lovely, sunny clementine/orange.

18 Cosmos/very dark blue is used to fill in the stick of her distaff. There is no shading here as it is quite a narrow strip of stitching, but bringing some of the peacock colours over into the left side of the image will help unite the image overall.

    Also, use a tiny little bit of this colour to add the bottom point of her spindle. Work it straight over the grass below. It needs to be only about one row of stitching wide, so it really wasn't worth leaving a gap in the grass.

19 Use foil/silver grey to outline the fibre of her distaff. The distaff holds the prepared fibre ready for spinning, and it was as vital a piece of equipment as the spindle itself. This distaff looks like it is dressed for flax, but she is sitting next to sheep, so I am going to assume that it is wool.

    Add some lines of texture to the wool on the distaff. I haven't drawn these into the pattern because they don't need to be precise: they are really just a sketch to indicate texture.

    Also, add an outline and some texture lines to the wool on the spindle. I have outlined only one side, and the texture lines go horizontally, unlike the vertical ones on the distaff, to indicate that the fibre has been wound around the shaft.

20 Next, fill in the wool on the distaff and spindle with lily/white, working the stitching in the same direction as for the outlines.

I also filled in the white of her eyes, to save myself the bother of threading another needle when working the next step.

Don't worry at this stage about the line of thread connecting the spindle and distaff. If it was added at this stage, it would be very difficult to work the background around it, so it will be almost the last thing that gets added, right over the top of everything else.

21 The strapping that holds the fibre to her distaff is worked by using a laid-and-couched work technique. Laid-and-couched work and trellis couching are quite rare in early period opus, but become increasingly common in post-Black Death pieces, because they are much quicker to work than is split stitch. In early period opus, they tend to be used for textural effect, as is the case here.

Work bands of laid work with paradise blue along the length of each strap, which is approached just like the threads being laid down for trellis couching. Don't worry if there is a slight curve in the thread; you can nudge it back into place with the couching. Then, use a single strand of gold to couch the blue down — it is the same principle as applied for the surface-couched gold used for The Riggisberg Lady project (*see* Chapter 4), but, instead of sewing a gold thread down with a silk one, here, we are sewing a bundle of silk threads down with a gold thread. Use very short lengths of the gold, threaded on a size 18 chenille needle, and make sure to enlarge the hole before pulling the thread through, to avoid shredding. Gold threads, even smooth-passing threads, aren't really designed for sewing through the fabric like this. It is one thing to sew smooth passing through an unadorned linen cloth with a reasonably low thread count, as one would for Elizabethan plaited-braid stitch, but this canvas is twice as fine and already quite heavily worked, so you need to proceed with care.

22 Outline the details of her face and her hands with cigar/very dark brown. I have used four strands for her face and three strands for her hands.

All princesses are entitled to lips as red as roses, so we are going to deviate from the standard opus mouth of one line of dark brown shaped to a disapproving frown and instead give her a nice dash of red instead. Use whichever shade from her dress that pleases you — I went for robin/bright red — worked as three tapered lines, to give a more realistic lip shape than standard.

23 Her hands and face are now filled in with two strands of allspice/warm brown.

Take care with her hands: the positions of her fingers are important to her task, and the last thing that you want is some finicky real-life spinster observing your beautifully finished work and telling you how wrong our girl's hands are. Spinning nerds are every bit as picky as are embroidery nerds!

The skin here is far less forgiving than the usual deathly white of standard opus, because covering a light colour with a dark one reveals every tiny gap.

24 Work the apples of her cheeks, taking care to touch the bottom of the eye and the side of the nose, so that her cheekbones are well defined. As usual, a line of stitching should connect from the outermost corner of the neck to the outer edge of the cheek apple, to establish the direction of the stitching when later filling in the neck and connect these different areas of the flesh.

25 Work her brow with all of the stitches running in one direction and packed closely together, connecting the brow with the side of her face by working upwards and across. Note how the side of the face and the nose both connect to the brow. Her brow should be smooth and unfurrowed, as, at this stage in our tale, she has not yet suffered the woe of being confined to a dungeon to spin wool into gold – she hasn't a care in world, just sitting in the sun, chilling with her peacock.

26 Fill in her nose and under her brows, again remembering to maintain a unified direction of stitching and always to split out of or into a previously made stitch. Also add to the stitching along the line connecting the neck and cheek, as shown.

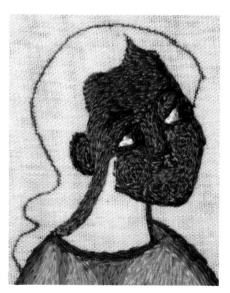

27 Place a smaller circle of stitching for her chin, and then work around the lower face by following the existing contours of her face, to fill in on the sides of the lower face and above the lips.

28 Lastly, fill in her neck. I worked up the initial line that connects her neck to her cheek, before establishing a line to follow the sinew of the neck and working around that stitching path until the neck was filled.

Once it was photographed, I realized that, despite taking extra care to fill all of the gaps, I could still see a few in the enlarged picture, so I went back and filled those in before doing her hair.

29 Her hair is worked in alternating double rows of black ebony and equator/deep red (which takes on a very fashionable purple tinge next to the black). It would be very tempting to tone her hair with brown, but this would blend into her face too much and wash out her complexion, whereas the reddish-purple tones enrich both her skin tone and her outfit.

30 The peacock is next. Obviously, he needs to be mostly blues and greens, but he also needs something to visually tie him to the rest of the image – using only blue and green would separate this image into two distinct halves. By using equator/deep red again for the outlining of his body and the centre of the eyes on his tail, chilli/dark red for his legs, and a tiny splash of clementine/orange for his beak, he is tied to the human figure, and, thus, the image becomes more harmonious.

Each of the central eyes of the tail feathers needs only a few stitches of red to be made in a tiny crescent shape: this may look too small at first, but we will build it up with successive layers of colour.

His actual eye is worked as just a few stitches of black ebony surrounded by an outline of white.

‹**31** He needs some stitching with cosmos/very dark blue next. Work around the edge of the tiny crescents of his tail, going around the lower half of each of the crescents only. Fill in his feet, and add a strip of about three rows of stitching to the underside edge of his wing.

The upper part of his neck should also be deep blue, but don't work a row of stitches along the lower edge, instead begin and end the rows of stitching at this edge, so not splitting anything right now. Finish each row with a half stitch, and don't let this edge go straggly, as the next layer of colour will split neatly out of these rows. You will need to work some fanning stitches to fill his neck at the base, where it grows wider, so always remember to split something as you work that area.

Leave a small gap around his eye as shown, which will be filled in with the next colour.

32 The next colour to use is the most perfectly peacocky shade called paradise blue/dark turquoise. We will use this colour again when we finish his tail, but for now fill in the area around his eye and then the area of his chest below the neck and above the leg.

Split the paradise blue/dark turquoise out of the cosmos/very dark blue stitching of the upper neck, so that they blend together.

When filling his chest, you don't need to obsess over matching the rows of stitching exactly to the rows of cosmos/very dark blue that you are splitting out of; as long as you work in the same direction and split out of the general area of dark blue, it will blend very well.

Finally, add another layer of colour to the eyes of his tail, this time continuing the stitching up to the top of each eye, to make a teardrop shape, as shown.

33 Next, we will use cappuccino/pale brown, but with a delicate touch. It is an important colour to add to his peacocky glory, but too much will make him look dowdy, and a dowdy peacock is a sad, sad peacock.

All that he needs is a single row of outline to the edge of his tail, two rows around each teardrop-shaped eye on the tail, a stripe of two or three rows on his upper back, where the wing meets the body, and some tiny little hollow circles on his wing, to add detail.

35 Fill the empty circles with tiny spots of underside-couched white gold no 5 smooth passing. This is quite fiddly to do, as you need to couch only the edges, but each spot requires only three or four stitches and adds a very subtle glimmer.

34 Lily/white is used to fill in his legs and wing. Although I have filled the legs in a circular fashion, I have worked the wing as a series of regular rows of stitching that simply duck under the pale-brown circles. This needs to be done with care, finishing each small row with a half stitch to round it out, but it will result in a nice, sleek wing.

36 Work his tail by using ten strands of paradise blue/dark turquoise (you can use a strand of 60 thread, which is basically ten strands of 6 thread, handily reeled for your convenience, instead of these strands of 6 thread) over two bars of very dark gold no 4 smooth passing, with the tail-feather surface-couching technique described in the accompanying box.

This is similar to the technique of or nue, in that a gold thread is decoratively couched with silk, but, whereas or nue uses many different colours of thread to create an image over the gold, the technique used here uses just one colour to create a decorative effect, so it is really more of a decorative surface-couching technique. In later crewel work, the same stitch is used with wool and known as burden stitch. In the early period of opus anglicanum, it seems to have been reserved for angels and peacocks. The basket-weave effect with little glints of gold shining through is quite effective for small areas, but it doesn't have the same stability as split stitch or underside couching, so it is not great for filling large areas.

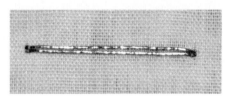

1 Start by laying down a double bar of very dark gold no 4 smooth passing across the area that you want to fill, making sure to tuck the gold neatly under any areas of silk around the edges. The couching stitches that we are going to use for this are a bit loosey-goosey, so don't be tempted to use the modern method of plunging the gold as a last step; this time, you want it fixed firmly in place before you begin. The silk will do enough sliding around on its own without letting the gold join in the fun.

2 We will be using ten strands of silk (again, the gorgeous shade that I have used here is called paradise blue). You can either measure out ten individual strands of 6 thread, or just buy a length of 60 thread instead, because it is quite easy to break 60 threads down when you want fewer strands for the body. For 60 thread, it does come with a very slight twist. If you give it a twist in the opposite direction, you will see that it is made from two strands of five threads; separate these two strands and lay them side by side to remove most of the twist, and, in the end, you get a fluffier bundle of ten threads.

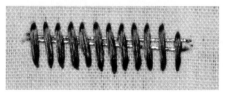

3 Couch the laid bars of gold with all ten strands of silk. Try to keep the stitches roughly perpendicular to the gold and spaced evenly – the gap should be around the same width as one bundle of ten threads. These couching stitches need to be overextended on each side of the gold bars, so that they will fit under the next row of gold without exposing any of the base canvas.

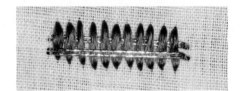

4 Lay down the next row of gold, again consisting of two adjacent bars, so that it covers the overextended points of the couching stitches of the previous row. It is better that the couching stitches be longer than necessary rather than shorter – remember that we don't want any white canvas showing at the end.

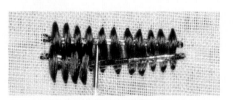

5 Couch this second double bar of gold by sliding the silk thread between the couching stitches used for the previous bar, to create a basket-weave effect. To achieve this, come up on the clean side of the bar, go over it, and then slide the needle down underneath the previous bar to ensure that the canvas is completely covered. If you find that your first row of couching bars are a bit overspaced, you might have to add a double bar here and there, as filler.

6 Once you have built up the required number of rows of gold and couching, finish off by working stab stitches between the couching stitches on the edges of the covered area, to fill the gaps on each side of the surface couching, as shown.

37 Transfer the background pattern on to the canvas if you haven't already done so. Because this pattern is quite large, there are areas where no pattern might appear or that are so small that imposing the continuation of the pattern would feel clumsy and intrusive. Sometimes it is best to fudge the smaller spaces a bit – for instance, between her face and her hand, I could have had a tiny bit of falcon sticking out at random, but it looks better to leave that space clean.

This design is very common across medieval Europe and is often found in brocade fabrics, as well as other media such as enamel and carving. Note that falcons were popular as symbols of nobility.

Before you begin to work the background, check the size of your pearls or beads, if you are using them, and adjust the circles to demark the points of the peacock's crown to fit, as necessary. Here I have drawn the crown to accommodate 3–4mm natural pearls.

Tips

Because many people write left to right, this set-up makes the stitching easier and leaves you with less to work in the opposite direction. If you are left-handed, you may find it easier to do the reverse. Always do the easiest part of the stitching first, so that you are more in the swing of things by the time you get to the more difficult parts.

38 Using the no 4 very dark gold smooth passing, begin by working the diagonals of the background pattern. I prefer to work laid-and-couched work horizontally, so I turned this piece on its side for this stage, so that my horizontal was vertical to the image, and then I first worked the left–right diagonals, including parts of the quatrefoils, as shown.

It is really important with this first stage to keep a neat edge and to stay vertical to the main image at all times. You may find it helpful to draw some vertical lines over the background-couching image to help to keep you on track if you tend to have difficulty with straight lines (this is best done with a contrast colour, so you don't confuse these lines with the image), but, if you have framed the canvas on the grain, you can simply follow the grain instead.

40› The heraldic falcons are a complicated shapes to fill, made more difficult by the need the 'draw' in the line of the wing with a line of couching. Because they are heraldic, I am going to show the process of filling two opposing birds at the same time, starting at two different points on the design.

The stitching of the left-hand bird was begun at the very tip of the wing, working up the slope of the wing until it was possible to work a section of couching right across to the top of the bird's head, before coming back and filling the shape of the upper wing.

The stitching of the right-hand bird started with the upper talon, working up and out across the chest and into the lower talon until

the couching touched the edge of the wing. Then the couching was worked back and forth across the lower body beneath the wing before expanding out to fill the tail.

39 Work the right–left diagonals next. Because you have already done some of the quatrefoils at the intersections, there is a lot less work to do on this pass. I am always convinced that my diagonals worked right to left are a little messier than those worked left to right, and I certainly feel that I have more trouble controlling the shapes as I stitch. However, if you are left-handed, you may find the opposite to be true for you, so work the quatrefoils when working in your easiest direction.

41 For the left-hand bird, couching picks up at the side of the neck, by working up along the breast until one long row spans the whole breast and down into the lower leg. Then the rows are worked out to move around the breast, before finishing at the raised leg.

For the right-hand bird, start his second stage of couching at the curve of the wing, working up the curve until the rows can stretch out to the top of his head, then work out to the point of the wing.

Starting and finishing complete rows at the edges of the wings gives the wing a shadowed outline, partly because there will be a neat row of ends and partly because the meeting of two separate rows will give a slightly deeper shadow than an ordinary underside couch. However, don't fret over the fact that this shadow will disappear where the wing and breast stitches line up – it is not meant to be a realistic depiction of a falcon – it is a rendition, an impression of a bird: your eye knows what a bird looks like, and the shadow of the wing is enough to tell the story.

Tips

The aim is always to work the largest stretch of stitching possible without having to plunge the ends of the sur-face thread. I work by eye, but you may find it helpful for the first few birds to draw the different stages on the background canvas.

It is important to keep a neat edge to the areas of couching and to keep all of the stitches vertical to the main image.

42 On the left-hand bird, work the tail next. By starting at the lower tip of the tail, I have worked back and forth until my last pass has gone down into the lower foot, and this has allowed me to finish the foot with the last of the thread.

On the right-hand bird, I have simply filled in the cavity of the chest. It can be quite tricky getting the last row of thread to sit straight when you are trying to wiggle it in between to others, and sometimes it is helpful to slide a stiletto between the gold threads once they are down, to get them to behave.

44 Once all of the very dark gold is filled in, there is quite a strong grid present. In some ways, this one is easier to fill than the circular background pattern used for Rapunzel, because it is bigger.

43 The final step is to fill in the beaks and claws, at which point you can move on to the counterpoint-couching filling.

45 Although we are using a slightly different shade of gold, white gold, for contrast, this is still a counterpoint-couching pattern, so remember to work at right angles to the stitching of the birds.

I began in the tiny gap where the grid meets in a quatrefoil. I doesn't matter which of the gaps you plump for, you just have to go back and fill the second one later. I then worked down and across the image, hitting the widest point possible while going back and forth, so I filled the area above the bird's heads before contracting the stitching to go between this bodies and flaring out again below their tails.

Notice that there are small gaps beneath wings and beaks that will require fixing later. Don't be tempted to bend your rows of couching to fit around these shapes to fill in these gaps as you go: keep straight and work to a line to get neat results.

Tips

If you are working with a standard slate frame with trestles, the best thing to do is to rotate the frame so that you are working in your most comfortable stitching direction. For this stage, I was working vertically, rather than from side to side as I had done with the birds, because I use a floor-standing frame and had to remind myself that I fill better if I start on the right-hand side of the image. Again, it is worth doing a few tests to find your best angle to work from, because it can have as much to do with your dominant eye as your dominant hand, and the two are not necessarily the same!

Take a moment to plan the route of your stitching in order to maximize the amount that you can work before having to start a new thread. I will show you how I filled a full diamond, but there are a lot of diamonds that are partial, so you will need to adapt your approach with each one.

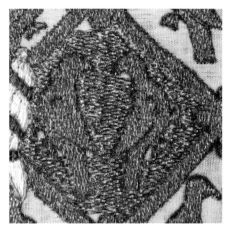

46 You can then work down the two outer sides of the diamond, as shown. These areas can get quite narrow, and you may end up just couching back and forth for a few stitches. Try to tuck your white gold under the very dark gold as closely as possible, but take care not to pierce any of the metal threads, in case they fray.

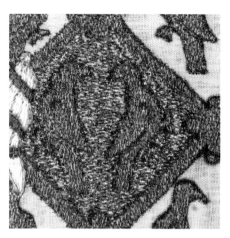

47 The final step is to fill all of the tiny gaps under beaks and feet and wings. This can be a bit of a fiddly job. I find it more satisfying to finish each square as a unit and then move on to the next one, but some people like to leave all of the tiny gaps to finish at once, so do what suits your temperament. Save all of the short ends of the white-gold passing from working the larger areas to use up for this step.

48 Once all of the gold is filled in, the piece does look rather glorious. If you choose to swap the background pattern, I think that the vine scroll, provided as an alternative pattern to trace, would work well with this image, because there is a lot of negative space to fill, but the background circles of the Rapunzel project (*see* Chapter 12) might look bitty unless you enlarge the pattern overall. I know that the pattern is meant to imitate an expensive gold brocade fabric, but I love how much it looks like wallpaper – then again, the same motifs recur time and again across medieval art, with the same repeat patterns being used for woven fabrics, embroidery, floor tiles and wall paintings, so maybe someone somewhere in fourteenth-century Europe did have this pattern on their walls, and they probably thought it was rather chic.

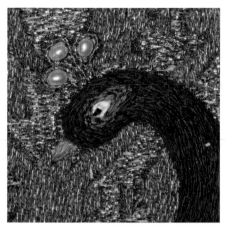

49 We need to work just a few finishing touches. The first thing to address is that the miller's daughter is currently holding a spindle and distaff but is spinning no thread, so that is the first thing to rectify. Ironically, since the king demanded that she spin gold, I am going to give her a thread of the next best thing – silver. Use a single strand of the silver passing, couched down by a single strand of the white silk – you can use a fine plied silk for this if you find it easier to work with, or a bit of filament: either is fine.

You are going to be couching across the top of the underside couching in places, so use the finest needle that you can, so that you don't pierce any of the metal – I used the beading needle, which will slide through the gaps, but it is a little difficult to aim.

50 The peacock needs his crown next, and for this I have used the dark gold twist for a small contrast in texture. A dark-blue-coloured passing or a little bit more silver would also look good. Again, it is worth checking the size of your pearls or beads before starting the twist couching, so that you can adjust the size of the circles to fit.

I have couched the twist with two strands of paradise blue/dark turquoise to bring this colour up into his crown, and the twist was couched as one continuous strand, starting at one corner before going up and around each circle of the crown. The technique is similar to that used for the points of the surface-couched crown in The Riggisberg Lady project (*see* Chapter 4).

51 Nestle a little pearl inside each circle, and our peacock is done.

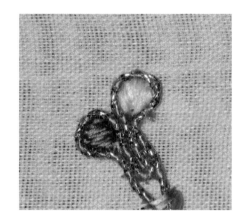

52 If you don't have pearls or beads, you can fill the circles with tiny spots of satin stitch, as shown, but it is best to do this before couching the twist; again, this use of satin stitch echoes what was done for one of horses of The Three Kings project (*see* Chapter 11). Make the satin stitch slightly bigger than the circle to be filled, so that the twist sits on top of it. Blue looks really good, and brings the colour upwards, but a spot of white could pass for a pearl, if you don't look too closely.

53 Once your final flourishes are in place, the piece is ready to mount (*see* Chapter 15) and possibly frame or assemble as part of a purse (*see* Chapter 16).

CHAPTER 14

SELFIE GIRL

TECHNIQUES

Having fun! Also female face, trellis couching, twill underside couching, working directly on to a coloured background

This final project is just a silly little design to remind you to have fun. Our character is an adaptation of one of the ladies in the *Codex Manesse*, a fourteenth-century German book of poetry that is wonderfully illustrated. As for the knight of The Small Knight project, she is worked directly on to red twill silk, so extra care must be taken to make sure that the stitches are close enough together, lest the silk show through.

Materials

Fabrics
- Double layer of fine ramie or linen fabric (60 to 80 count), 20cm × 20cm (about 8in × 8in)
- A piece of red twill silk of about the same size as the double-layer ramie or linen fabric, as the top layer of the silk–ramie (or –linen) canvas

Needles
- Size 8 crewel needle
- Size 18 chenille needle

Threads
- Tram silk thread, one 10g spool each in the following shades:
  - acorn
  - dark cream
  - dark olive
  - fuchsia
  - green
  - light cream
  - pale blue
  - pink
  - purple
  - rust
  - teal
  - turquoise
  - yellow
    Please note that one whole spool of each colour is more than adequate for the working of this project: any thread remaining can be used for the working of several other projects.
- Como silk thread, one 10g spool in the following shades:
  - black
  - copper
    Please note that one whole spool of each colour is more than adequate for the working of this project: any thread remaining can be used for the working of several other projects.
- Plied silk thread, gold-coloured – 60/2nm in gold *or* DeVere Yarns 36 thread in 86 straw
- 2/5nm spun-silk thread, at least 1m (about 40in), in white
- Please note that, if you purchase one whole 10g spool of this 2/5nm thread, this is more than adequate for the working of this project: any thread remaining can be used for the working of several other projects.
- Benton & Johnson smooth passing no 4, at least 5m (about 16½ft) in very dark gold
- Benton & Johnson smooth passing no 5, at least 5m (about 16½ft) in silver
- Please note that I have used no 4 and no 5 smooth-passing threads in very dark gold and silver left over from the Rapunzel and Rumpelstiltskin projects (*see* Chapter 12 and Chapter 13, respectively). Feel free to use leftover passing threads of your choice to complete this project.
- Strong linen thread, for couching
- Lacing thread

Additional materials
- Beeswax, for waxing linen thread

A few fun pieces

In a similar vein to this project, Brenda Scarman's piece from an embroidery class is again adapted from the *Codex Manesse*. The featured lady is sitting by the river stitching while her husband fishes; her sampler spells out *stultus puer* – Latin for 'stupid boy'. This piece has been worked with silk split stitch and underside couching, with a touch of trellis couching for the fishes.

These two pieces, which are two sides of the same purse, are also adapted from manuscripts: the day side is adapted, as for Brenda's stupid boy, from the *Codex Manesse*, but it had cats instead of hawks. The night side is adapted from a medieval health manual, illustrating the importance of regular nookie for good health.

1 Mark out the design on the triple-layer, silk-topped canvas.

2 The first step is to fill in the shelf that our selfie lady is leaning on, and, for this, we are going to use a little bit of trellis couching, the same as used for Rapunzel's book, but it is worked over a slightly larger area. Large areas of trellis are used a lot in late-period opus anglicanum as a quick-and-dirty filler for backgrounds and architectural elements, but this technique tends to be used for smaller details in the early period of opus. However, including a smartphone in the composition isn't strictly authentic, so I think that we can take a few liberties with the stitch choice as well.

Use six strands of the green tram silk in the needle at once for this stage, as the aim is to fill the shape as quickly as possible, and work huge, parallel stitches, working from left to right. Remember that this isn't satin stitch, so come up practically right next to where you went down, and keep almost all of the silk at the front of the canvas. This area will be filled in within a few minutes – you will probably spend more time threading your needle than you will sewing for this part.

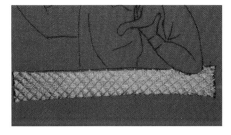

3 You could use a flat filament silk for working the trellis bars, but it can be a bit slippery, so I have used a twisted and plied silk thread. Surviving examples of trellis couching, such as on the Clare Chasuble, include plied silk, and it does make life a little easier, but in truth you need only a few metres for this job, and it is the kind of thing that you raid your workbox for rather than buying anything specific – it doesn't even need to be gold, whatever colour tickles your fancy will do fine. I have used a gold 60/2nm weaving silk from The Handweavers Studio & Gallery, because I tend to keep it in stock for all kinds of odd jobs, but I have listed the closest alternative of the DeVere Yarns silk thread as well.

Lay down your trellis over the green silk. You may find that the green silk threads will have wandered around a bit, because their span is quite long, so you can use the trellis to nudge them back into line. In truth, I have nudged mine too far the other way and exposed my drawing at the top, but it is not something that I am going to worry about, as I intend to later put an outline around this area of trellis couching.

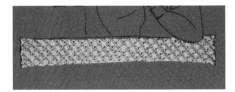

4 Use the same gold thread to couch the trellis at the intersections. You can use a third colour if you want to, but I have decided to keep it simple this time.

I love how much this looks like a cushion, slightly raised from the surface, which is more effective when you work directly on to the background rather than applying the piece as a slip. Trellis couching is often used for the rendering cushions in medieval pieces.

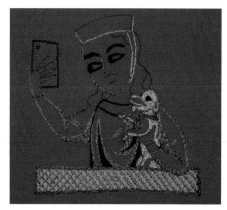

5 Use four strands of tram silk for working the outlines.

A double outline of dark olive needs to be added around the trellis area. Also, give the dog a small collar worked with two rows of green, leaving a tiny gap between them for later adding a row of underside couching – our puppy needs some sparkle.

Use purple for outlining her dress and phone, with some shading being included for some of the dress outlines.

Use acorn for outlining her sleeves, skin, and the little dog, and pink for outlining her headdress and the tongue of the little dog.

Finally, use a quarter strand of black Como silk for the eyes. She is fashionable, so she needs smoky eyes, and I have worked her brows in this thick black as well, as is the current fashion with young ladies who are obsessed with selfies.

6 Continue using four strands of tram silk to add the first layer of colour and shading to her clothing.

Fuchsia is used for the sleeves of her underdress. I am following the shading of the original manuscript illustrations, so I am working from a fixed point of light at the top left, just as you would when painting, so the shadows are deeper near her armpits.

Teal is used next to add the subsequent layer of shadow on her overdress, again with the deeper colours to the right of the image, away from the point of light.

Use four strands of dark cream for filling in the dog's body and two strands for his face. He is going to be a sandy-coloured pup, so, although this is a light colour, it will be the shadowy part of his body.

7 Next, we need to add the middle layer of colour and shading to her clothing, again by using four strands of thread.

Use pink for filling in her sleeves. Although the upper arm has baggy drapery to allow movement, the cloth over the forearm is really the only part of this outfit that is closely fitted, so it is important to show off her slender wrists. As such, take care to use the pink to model the shape of the arm below the cloth.

Turquoise is the next layer of colour for the cyclas, and here no attempt is made to show the shape of the body beneath: it is all about the drapery. Even with figures depicted in fitted gowns, there is really no attempt to depict the breasts, so there is nothing to see here.

Remember to follow the direction of the previously made stitches and to always split out of and into the existing rows of stitching.

Ladies' clothing

Our young lady is wearing the kind of dress fashionable in the four-teenth century, called a cyclas or sideless surcoat (or surcote), which is basically a long, shapeless pinafore worn over a long gown with tightly cuffed sleeves. This is primarily worn for warmth, and the style is about graceful, flowing drapery. It was worn by both sexes. Selfie girl loves her cyclas – it is bang on trend for the fourteenth-century 'It girl'!

BLENDING

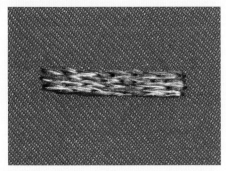

This blending is something that I use mostly for animals, as it gives a furry, brindled look. Here is the test patch that I did of threads of acorn and dark cream blended together, which I considered using for the darker areas of little Fido.

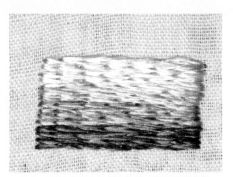

And here is a demonstration of blending with the shades used for our girl's blue overdress, from bottom to top: purple and teal, teal and turquoise, turquoise and pale blue, and pale blue and light cream. This would be a lovely effect to use for water, or, if you wanted to depict blue jeans in opus, mixing two blues could give the look of denim.

Finally, this is a piece that I did many years ago with some naturally dyed silks that came in only about twelve colours, so I added some variation by blending the colours on the dapples of the horse. It came out looking exactly like the strawberry-roan pony that I had when I was little.

8› Use pale blue to fill in the cyclas and light cream for the highlights on her pink sleeves. It may seem odd to use a shade of white as a highlight for pink, but the pink is very pale, and, in this case, the red silk below and proximity to the pink actually makes the cream take on a slight blush. However, if you find the cream too stark, you could try mixing it with some pale pink, as we are going to do for the stitching of the dog in the next step.

Also, use some of the light cream for her headdress. There is no attempt at shading or shaping here: just keep the fillet (the top part) and the barbette (the chin strap) as pale as possible – clean white linen is a sign of wealth and refinement. Notice that I haven't worked all of the way to the top of the fillet – that comes later.

9 I wanted a very subtle shading on the dog, so I have blended two strands of dark cream with two strands of light cream, which has made a quite subtle difference, allowing me to add highlights.

Blending two colours is a good way to widen a narrow colour palette, but it is a more modern thing to do, as it gives a marled appearance to the silk.

Working with Como silk

One strand of copper Como silk splits down easily into four, but these quarter strands, when rubbed along their lengths, break down into another four strands, of which we are going to use two for the flesh. Normally, for Como silk, one such strand is sufficient for the stitching of skin, but the red background here is harder to cover effectively, so it is best to sacrifice a little finesse in this case.

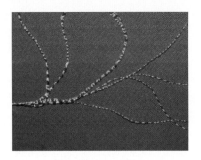

10 I was originally going to use a proper pale-and-pasty opus skin colour for selfie girl, but then I realized that no true fashionista would dream of forgoing her regular spray tan, hence the copper skin.

Use an eighth of a strand of copper Como silk for her the stitching of her hands. They are quite straightforward to do: just work every row of stitching out from the wrist.

11 If you are going to go to the trouble of having a spray tan, you might as well get some acrylic nails and a spot of filler in your lips while you are at the salon. (And it gives more time to catch up on all the gossip.) Use whichever thread colours you please.

Original opus never bothers with nails, or lips for that matter, but rules are to be bent.

12 She will start to look considerably less demonic once she has proper skin, so let's start with her cheeks. Remember to make the apples nice and high, hitting the lower eyelids and the side of the nose. She says that she will consider getting some work done when she needs it, but please don't hurry things along by giving her saggy skin.

13 Split out from her cheek and work up the side of her face into and across her forehead. If she gets frown lines, she intends to Botox them, so make a straight line across her brows with no dip between the eyes.

Remember to pack the stitches closely and tightly together, and always split something.

14 Split out from her forehead to go down her nose, around the tip and split back into the adjacent cheek. Continue building on this line until you can join up her nose with the arch of her underbrow. The underbrow on the right as we look at the piece should in turn be split into the side of her face to create a seamless (and wrinkle-free, thank you very much) span of flesh.

Fill in her other underbrow while you are at it.

15 Work her chin by splitting out from the cheek, following the jawline, and then working around the mouth and into a smaller spiral for the chin. Work the upper lip by bringing the top of the spiral down to meet it, and then fill in the lower cheeks by splitting out of the apples and into the chin.

Finally, fill in any corners and gaps.

I am wondering whether perhaps she needs her lips being made a little bigger, but the best thing to do is to finish everything and then reconsider, rather than jumping in straight away.

16 When filling in her neck, remember to work diagonally as if following the sinews.

17 I wanted lots of body in her hair (I don't think that it is all natural – she has most likely had extensions), so I went up to working with six strands of yellow and rust, and I gave it far more oomph than in the original sketch. And, well, it just had to be blonde, babe.

18 Let's add some underside couching next. Silver no 5 smooth passing is used for the brick-pattern underside couching for the smartphone and very dark gold no 4 smooth passing for the twill underside couching for her collar and cuffs and the dog's collar. You could instead use a coloured passing here – I was very tempted by some baby blue, but, on the whole, the gold balances out the yellow in her hair.

19 The final touch is to finish her fillet. Often this fashionable piece of fourteenth-century headgear is shown as pleated all the way around, but the German manuscripts, such as the *Codex Manesse*, tend to show a funny little frill all the way along the top. Rather than trying to embroider the frill, I am going to add it as a texture – this is not strictly an authentic medieval stitch, although something similar is used in medieval appliqués. All that I have done is surface couch a length of 2/5nm silk (I call it fluffy caterpillar silk, because it is very strokeable) and pull the silk out into a little puff between each couching stitch, to give the effect of a textured frill along the top. It doesn't really matter whether you use a linen or a silk thread for the couching, just as long as it is white.

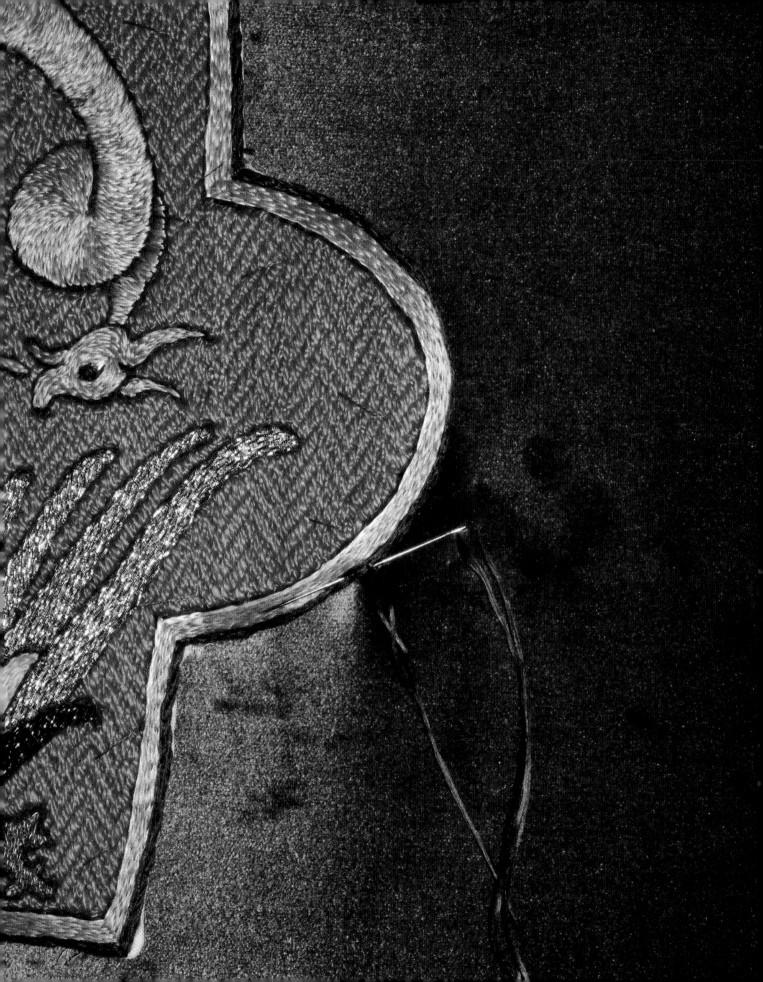

CHAPTER 15

SLIPS

A slip is a piece of embroidery that is cut out after its completion and is stitched to another, larger piece of fabric, to back and to mount it. Although some opus anglicanum pieces were mounted as slips, often opus was worked directly on to velvet, or twill silk, and frequently the work was so huge, as in the case of a cope, that no background at all was seen. However, few of us these days will be working a full-scale liturgical cloak, so being able to mount the work as a slip is a useful way to finish a piece neatly for display.

It is a good idea to start with a simple shape such as that of The Three Kings project (*see* Chapter 11) or the St Michael Syon Cope-inspired project (*see* Chapter 7) before moving on to the more complex figures and formats, which have much more complicated and wobblier edges.

I always find this step of mounting a slip intimidating, though, and find myself putting it off, because there really is something very scary about going near a piece of embroidery with a pair of scissors…

VELVET SELECTION

Before you can do anything, you must choose a velvet upon which to mount the embroidery. Let's go through the available options, shown in the accompanying photo:

- The brown stuff is what is commonly sold as silk velvet by modern vendors. Frankly, it is horrible: avoid it – it is not even silk, it is around 78-per-cent rayon. The structure of velvet is composed of a woven background, which you don't see, and a fluffy pile, which is the bit that you do see and feel. This 'silk' velvet is so-called because the woven part at the back is silk, but the face of the fabric is 100-per-cent rayon; it is made this way to be usable for a technique called devoré, where a resist is painted on to the fabric's face and an acid is then applied that eats away the rayon pile to create patterns. On the whole, this 'silk' velvet is completely unsuitable for our purpose, because it is too flimsy by far.

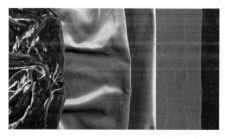

Velvets come in different types, and not all are suitable for opus. Here is a selection of rayon-based 'silk' velvet, real silk velvet, vintage silk velvet, cotton velvet and wool–mohair velvet (from left to right).

- Second from the left is the silk velvet that I have used for all but one of the projects in this book. It has a silk pile and a sturdy cotton back (medieval silk velvets often had a linen back, again because the logic was to not waste silk where it won't be seen) and is gorgeous for the mounting of slips. (However, I am reliably informed that it is a nightmare to photograph – there has been much complaining about it.)
- In the centre is a vintage silk velvet, kindly given to me by Bess Chilver, that has both silk pile and a silk back, and the pile is a very short pile. If you are lucky enough to find some, buy it at once, but be aware that it is much

more difficult to sew with than the cotton-backed velvet, as the vintage velvet resists the needle.

⊰ Second from the right is a cotton velvet. It is very dull compared to the silks, but, if you can't get silk or can't afford it, cotton velvet is widely available and relatively cheap. Be aware that velvet and velveteen are not the same thing, though.

⊰ The blue fabric on the far right is a wool–mohair velvet, which has a much duller, more matt pile (it also picks up cat hair like you wouldn't believe). Although this fabric is period appropriate, modern wool velvets are produced primarily for upholstery and therefore have a much denser pile that can make this type of velvet fabric unsuitable for mounting embroidery as a slip. I tried mounting The Cherub piece on this particular fabric and had to pick him off again, so check the pile density before making a decision.

Identifying real silk velvet

There are several ways to tell real silk velvet from 'silk' velvet.

- Price: If you pay more than £20 per metre for the rayon stuff, you are being ripped off, but, if you find a proper silk velvet for around £100 per metre, you have got a bargain.
- Drape: Look how wrinkly the example brown stuff is and compare it with the much stiffer fabric next to it. The mostly rayon 'silk' velvet is also very light in weight, having almost no real substance.
- Shine: 'Silk' velvet has a very cheap shine, yet silk velvet is lustrous, rather than shiny. Also, if you know what silk feels like to the hand, this feels nothing like that.

STEP-BY-STEP INSTRUCTIONS

1 The first step is to cut away the majority of the background canvas from around your embroidered piece. You need to trim down to about one centimetre of background canvas all around the embroidery.

Use your tiny embroidery scissors for this. If you slip with a large pair of dressmaking scissors, you can do fifteen to eighteen centimetres (about six to seven inches) of damage in an instant. If you slip with the teeny weeny embroidery scissors, the most that you can do is a couple of centimetres (or an inch) of damage.

But you are *not* going to slip. Breathe. Also, lock the cat/dog/children out of the room for five minutes, just to be on the safe side.

2 We are going to be turning what is left of the background canvas down on to the back of the work, so we don't want a lot of bulk back there. Trim away the back layer of the exposed double-layer background canvas; you can take it right down to the edge of the stitching, as the stitches are packed so tightly, there will be no fraying, and that raw edge will very soon be enclosed.

3 Turn the remaining layer of background canvas down and then roughly whip stitch it to the back of the embroidery, by taking the threaded needle through the stitching on the back of the work. Take care to make your stitches shallow, so that they don't show through on the front.

I cannot stress this enough – use a silk thread for working the whip stitch. I keep 60/2nm spun silk to hand just for this purpose. Silk will resist penetration by other fibres, which can tangle and knot and pull your stitching out of shape. Silk thread slides through silk.

You will need to carefully cut into the inner corners, to allow the background canvas to fold fully and flatly to the back of the work; don't worry about the raw edges in the corners, as, when you come to sew the slip down, you can put a few extra stitches there, right in the corners. Trim the excess canvas away from the outer corners, to avoid bulk, and again fold the canvas neatly and flatly to the back of the work.

4 Aim to fold as much white canvas as you can underneath the embroidery and out of sight without losing the edge of the embroidery. There will always be the odd spot where canvas will peek out at the front, but that can be dealt with when you sew the slip down. The goal is to fold under 99 per cent of the background canvas, to save time and effort later.

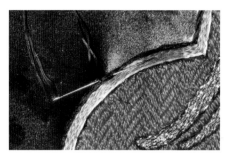

5 Stretch your background on a frame, without any rolling or folding if you are using a roller frame – you want the whole of the background on show. The background should be held flat, but not stretched tightly. If you sew your slip to a tight canvas, there will be shrinkage when you remove the background from the frame. It is a bit of a juggling act, but you want the slip and the canvas to be at about the same tension.

If you are using velvet, give it a good brush to make sure that all of the pile lies in the same direction before you begin: an old-fashioned natural-bristle brush is best for this purpose.

6 Tack the slip down on to your nice, flat velvet. All you need to achieve this is a few big stitches, to stop things from moving around, as velvet is terrible stuff for moving. Again, this should be done with a silk thread to avoid damage to the embroidery, but the colour doesn't matter at all. I used green because it was what came out of my sewing box first.

At this stage, you can see that there are still a few white edges showing.

7 Use a small, neat hem stitch to secure the slip, and use the same colour of silk as used on the edge of the piece being mounted as a slip to sew the slip down. This way, you can bite with your needle right into the edge of the piece without having to worry about the stitch showing too much. You can even work a few sneaky satin stitches if you need to, to completely cover a stubborn bit of white.

In this case, the edge is all of one colour all the way around, but, with most projects, you will need to change the colour of your thread as you go, to match the colour of the edge at that part of the slip.

Background-colour choice

I am using green velvet for the St Michael Syon Cope-inspired piece, because the filler panels on the Syon Cope are green, but that is me taking a modern liberty, as nearly all of the medieval velvet that was used for opus was red. The almost ubiquitous choice of red velvet in the Middle Ages was less to do with taste than with expense. Opus anglicanum was expensive, so you wanted to mount it on the most expensive fabric, which was silk velvet, in the most expensive colour, which was red. When I say that the choice of red was about expense, it wasn't about economy – it was about showing that you didn't need to economize.

8 Tuck any bits of white background canvas that still show to the underneath of the slip as you go along, using your tool of choice.

When the slip is sewn down, always remove your tacking stitches from the back of the work, to avoid damaging the embroidery on the front.

There are endless options for where you can mount your embroidered slips; here, you can see that Liz Elliot has added her Luttrell Psalter beastie as a slip to an elegant velvet evening bag.

Tips

I have a mellor and a stiletto for this very purpose, but, in truth, most of the time, I use the edge of my scissors to shove any errant white bits out of the way, and it works just as well as any fancy tool.

Sometimes you will find that the bit that you want to hide, especially when it is on or in a corner, just won't stay put long enough for you to sew it under. In these cases, it can really help to skip ahead a little, say, by the length of three or four stitches, and firmly anchor the part of the slip in front of the problem area before then working back to it. By anchoring on each side of your problem area, you give the background canvas there less chance to sneak back into view.

You can also use your scissors or stiletto to carefully give anything still showing a good shove underneath the embroidery once the stitches are in place. (I find the mellor is too blunt and chunky for sliding underneath stitches.)

CHAPTER 16

ASSEMBLING A PURSE

For several of the projects featured in the previous chapters, I have mentioned the option of mounting the finished piece as part of an embroidered purse. In this chapter, we will work through the assembly of such an almoner's purse or aumoniere; here, I am using the finished embroidered pieces of the Rapunzel and Rumpelstiltskin projects (see Chapter 12 and Chapter 13, respectively).

1 Because I will line my purse with silk, I will back the front and back pieces of embroidery (in this case, they are squares) with a panel of wool cloth – you could instead use felt. Cut this backing fabric to the size of the embroidery pieces.

STEP-BY-STEP INSTRUCTIONS

Materials

- Two pieces of opus anglicanum embroidery of the same dimensions, one for the front and one for the back of the purse
- Wool cloth or felt, for backing the embroidery pieces
- Various silk threads: 60/2nm and 30/2nm spun-silk threads and Como silk threads were used for this example
- Benton & Johnson smooth passing no 6, at least 70cm (about 28in) needed for *each* tassel: gold and silver were used for this example
- Silk cloth such as silk crêpe *or* silk tablet weaving (to edge the top of the purse)
- Silk lining
- Linen thread, for assembly
- Sharp scissors
- Chenille needle
- Hair tie *or* Hugo's amazing tape (optional)
- Pliers (optional)
- Stiletto, for making eyelet holes

The backing-fabric colour doesn't matter, as it will never be seen, but I have used very, very dark green because this fabric was at the top of the scraps box and of roughly the right size. The wool isn't there to protect the back of the embroidery; rather, it is there to protect the silk lining, as well as the hand that dips into the purse – you might have noticed by now that the rear side of underside couching worked with metal threads is a bit abrasive.

Cut out each of the pieces of embroidery as you would at the start of the process for mounting a slip (see Chapter 15), leaving around a fifteen-millimetre edge all around for the front layer of the ramie or linen canvas and trimming the back layer of the canvas right back to the edge of the stitching. For each piece of embroidery, place one square of backing fabric on to the back surface, then fold over the 15mm canvas edges along each side in turn (folding the fabric neatly at the corners as shown), and roughly tack down these canvas edges by stitching through them and into the backing fabric only with linen thread. We now have two panels that will later be assembled to form the purse.

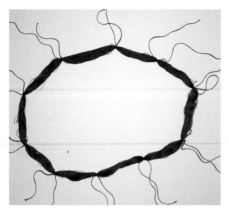

2 The next job is to make the silk-thread tassels.

Winding the thread for this many tassels would be a pain if you were to make them individually the way that I was taught in primary school, so I am going to cheat. Wind your silk into one large skein, taking care not to make it too thick: tassels on purses should be on the skinny side; if they look like curtain tie-backs, you have gone too far. Next, using a thread of a matching colour, tie the skein tightly at eight- to ten-centimetre (about three- or four-inch) intervals, leaving long tails for the ties, with which you will eventually anchor the tassels to the purse: I have used turquoise blue Como silk for tying the blue tassels and yellow Como silk for tying the gold tassels. If you have a yarn swift, you can use it for fast winding, as well as for unwinding, by clamping it horizontally – I clamp mine to a bannister, but the back of a chair works too.

I am using 60/2nm spun-silk thread in teal and 30/2nm spun-silk thread in gold – the difference in weights doesn't matter as much as does the colour. Both of these silks are sold in ten-gram spools for weaving, so they are more economical to use than trying to make tassels from expensive embroidery threads.

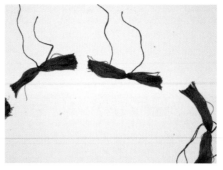

3 Now, cut through the skein of wound silk threads at an equal distance between two adjacent ties, working your way around the skein, and – voila! – you have the makings of many tiny tassels. As you can see, I made ten bundles of tassel threads from this skein. (I was actually aiming for twelve, but I am not great at measuring.)

5 Take some of the leftover tassel silk and use a doubled thread to tie a knot around the top end of your tassel-thread bundle. Try not to place this tie too low down, as you don't want this bit of thread to show and it is purely functional: you should eventually be covering it with the decorative cap of the tassel.

You may find it handy to wrap the dangly bits of the tassel in a hair tie while you work, just to keep them under control. Hugo's amazing tape is even better if you have some: it is a clear plastic tape that sticks to itself and is almost infinitely reusable. If you can find some, it would be a good purchase: it is pretty much the only thing that stops filament silks from tangling up in storage.

4 Cut about 70cm of gold or silver no 6 smooth passing, knot the end, and place the knot in the centre of the bundle, as shown. Fold the bundle of tassel threads over the knot to enclose it.

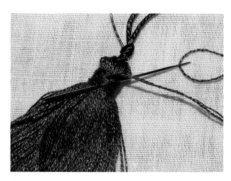

6 Wrap the doubled thread tightly around the top of the tassel several times, making it as solid and compressed as possible, before stitching the end underneath the wound threads to anchor it.

The loose ends of this tie can be left to hang down as part of the tassel.

7 Now, you need a needle on the end of your gold or silver passing thread, so thread this on to a suitably sized chenille needle (remember to put only the very end of the metal passing thread through the needle to avoid damage).

The first step is to make a loop of metal passing thread around the top of the tassel, to begin to encircle the top of the tassel-thread bundle and the suspension thread or hanging cord (that is, the long tails of the tying thread). Loop the metal passing thread under itself as shown, much as you would for working blanket or buttonhole stitch.

8 Next, work a row of seven or eight buttonhole stitches over this loop and around the top of the tassel – how many stitches will depend on how thick your tassel is. For the initial row, you need to pierce the top of the tassel slightly when making each stitch, just picking up a thread or two of the silk thread, as shown, to stop the buttonhole stitches from riding up the suspension thread.

9 Continue to work your way around the head of the tassel making buttonhole stitches by taking the needle behind both threads of the adjacent stitch of the previous row (that is, the two threads that twist around the back of the loop immediately above it), to create a knitted look, as shown. The stitching will try to ride up, so you may have to pull the previous stitching down in order to take the needle and thread under it.

12 This detached-buttonhole-stitch variation tends to twist around, as you can see here, because you go through the lowest loop of thread that travels from one stitch to the next, so you get a slight stagger at every stitch.

However, I like the knitted look that you get from crossing the loops by working the buttonhole stitches as described earlier.

10 This knitted-look variation lines up the stitches, one below the other, so you get ribs like those on a knitted jumper.

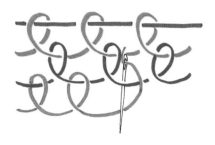

11 If you take the needle behind only the lower loop of the adjacent stitch of the previous row instead, in the style of detached buttonhole stitch, as shown, it will work just as well and still be very attractive.

Tassels

Medieval people loved tassels on a purse, and if you are making the medieval equivalent of the designer-bag form of arm candy, you want as many tassels as you can reasonably cram into the available space, plus a few extra for good luck. I opted for twenty-four in total, and, because more is most definitely more when it comes to medieval fashion, I am aiming for using more than one colour. They didn't do minimalism back then!

There were some ludicrously complicated tassels on medieval purses that are a whole other craft in themselves, and some purses featured small embroidered knobs instead of tassels. I am not much of a passementerie geek and am going to use a form of tassel that is essentially embroidery based.

13 Once you have covered the head of the tassel with stitching, push the needle under the edge of the metal passing thread and right through the head of the tassel so that it comes out at the top, as shown.

14 You now need to push the needle back down, again going through the head of the tassel, so that the needle comes out in the middle of the bundle of threads. You may need to keep a pair of pliers handy at this point, to help you to pull the needle through.

15 Trim the metal passing thread down so that it will later be concealed by the fall, or the bundled threads, of the tassel – you can trim it a lot closer than I am showing here.

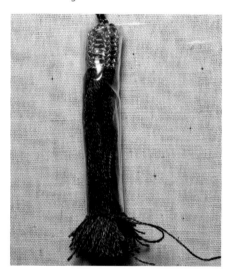

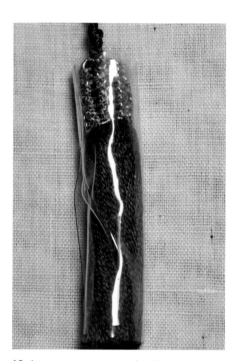

16 Your tassel should now be wearing a fancy little knitted hat. The final step is to trim the bottom so that the bundled threads lie reasonably straight, but I like to wait until all the of tassels are done and to trim them all at once, so I can get them all of the same length. Ish.

17 My biggest problem with tassel-making is trimming the bottom to be properly flat: I always seem to get it slightly uneven. I recently discovered that, if you take a piece of Hugo's amazing tape and cut it to the exact length of your tassel and then wrap each tassel tightly in the tape as shown, it can act as a guide to get the correct length. Use the same piece of tape for every tassel and they should come out quite even.

‹19 Once all of your tassels are completed, sort them into pairs and tie the hanging cords together about two centimetres (about one inch) from the ends – you need to be able to separate the tassels a little bit when you sew the purse sides and attach the edging braid at a later stage.

18 As you can see, wrapping the tassel in this way also gives a much tighter bundle of thread than does tying or holding the tassel falls for cutting, so that you get a really clean edge, as you can see here. It is not a very period solution, but it works very well.

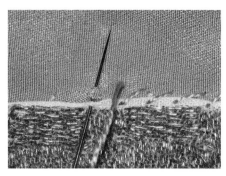

20 You can use a piece of silk tablet weaving around the top of your purse, but in this case I am going to use a piece of silk cloth. I have chosen a simple dull-gold colour that tones with the background – this one is a heavy silk crêpe from Beckford silks. You want something with body and a bit of diagonal movement such as a satin or crêpe; something too stiff like a taffeta won't work very well.

Cut two rectangles, each about a couple of centimetres (or an inch) or so wider than the top of the front and back panels and about thirteen centimetres (about five inches) deep.

First, fold the silk fabric over the top edge of one panel, leaving a generous couple of centimetres (about an inch) of overlapping fabric on what will be the inside of the purse. The aim is to whip stitch the silk fabric to the top of the panel from the reverse side (inside); this allows you to whip stitch the silk fabric as close as possible to the upper edge of the embroidery. Using whip stitch can feel a little sloppy alongside such precise embroidery, but it was often used in the construction of medieval things.

To make sure that my stitching lined up against the top edge of the panel, I folded the excess fabric down over the front of the embroidery to keep it out of the way, and to make sure that the seam lies as tightly as possible along the top edge.

At this point, you should have a single layer of silk fabric sewn to the top of each panel, with the fabric extending several centimetres upwards above each panel. (Later, the drawstrings for closing the purse will be threaded through this fabric.)

Attach the other piece of silk to the other panel in exactly the same way.

Use a silk thread for sewing the silk. Note that linen or cotton thread will only give you trouble, because they will fight with the silk at every stitch: silk into silk is always easier. I have used the same 30/2nm gold thread that I used for some of my tassels.

21 Working from the front of the panel now, stitch along the uppermost edge of each panel and into the silk fabric extending above the top of the panel to add an extra row of small whip stitches for stability, as shown. You could probably get away without this layer of stitching, if you are feeling lazy, but there is nothing that I hate more than doing repairs, so I tend to over-engineer with construction to save the bother later.

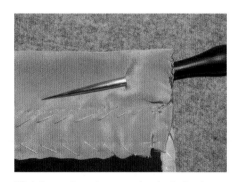

23 It is much easier to make the holes for the drawstring now. Alternatively, you could make the silk at the top of the purse into a tube for the drawstrings, instead of following steps 20–22.

You want four eyelets across the top of each panel – four allows you to insert a double lace properly, but five won't work: it has to be an even number.

22 Returning to the back of the panel, fold in the edges of the silk-fabric rectangle, to double the fabric here enough to hide the raw edges, then sew it down to the back of the panel, again by using whip stitches worked through the silk fabric and into the backing fabric of the panel. Do the same for the other panel. Sew up the edges of these folded short sides as well, to stop them from unfolding and moving – don't be too tempted to pin the sides and sew them later, because you will probably stab yourself with the pin while manhandling the purse. Pins were not for sewing in medieval times – they were for holding finished clothing together.

Don't worry if your silk is a little narrower than the top of the purse (you can see that mine leans in a little), but don't make it wider.

Measure your two halves to make sure that the silk is level: it is much more difficult to adjust it later.

The medieval way of making eyelets is to make a hole in the cloth without severing any of the woven threads, so a lovely pointy stiletto is vital. Insert it, then wiggle and twist until you have enlarged the hole as far as you can. I find that it helps to make the hole about half of the intended size from one side and then to reinsert the stiletto to work on the hole from the other side. This not only prevents too much distortion, but you also seem to get a better hole.

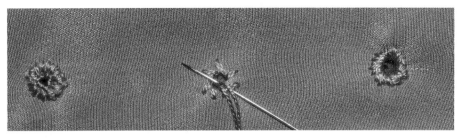

24 How you sew around the eyelets makes a difference. I think that my first instinct is always to use buttonhole stitch, but, as you can see from the sample on the left, buttonhole stitch actually pulls in the side of the hole and makes it smaller. We want the hole to be bigger, so it is best to just go around and around the edge.

For the middle hole, you can see that the first stage is simply to go around the edge of the hole with about eight stitches, pulling each one tight to keep the hole open. Then, on the right, you can see where I have done a second pass to neaten and firm things up.

25 Once the tops of the panels are dealt with, the next step is to place the paired tassels around the edge of one panel (it doesn't matter which one), stitching them firmly into place on the back – I like to stitch through the knot that holds both tassels of each pair together.

Be sure to leave a little bit of play at the top of each tassel. There needs to be enough room not only to sew the purse together but also for the tassels to interact with the edging braid that will be attached a bit later.

26 Stitching this the conventional modern way, by arranging the purse panels and holding and stitching them inside out and then turning the purse the right way out, simply isn't going to work, because the embroidery is so stiff. Instead, you sew it together the right way out.

Use a sturdy double thread – I have used the gold 30/2nm silk as used for the tassels, but linen thread is good too. Rather than starting at the top edge, begin at one of the bottom corners so that everything lines up properly. Neatly whip stitch along the edges, trying not to clip the edge of the embroidery.

The tassels are a pain at this point, as they are easily tangled in the sewing thread, but you just have to work around them.

Try not to sew the tassels inside the purse; if you do, you will feel very foolish!

27 Sew up one side of the purse from the bottom corner to the very top of the silk cloth, and also sew all the way across the bottom. Sew up the other side of the purse from the bottom corner to the top of the embroidery, but leave the upper part, where you get to the silk cloth, open. It is impossible to have sewn the silk cloth to the top of the embroidery in a presentable fashion (*see* step 21), so you need to cover the join with an edging braid.

My first three-strand edging plait is of copper and yellow Como silk threads, and you can see here that I have stitched it over the join between the embroidery and the silk cloth to cover it; this needs to be done after the main part of the purse is sewn together but before that final top join of the silk cloth is completed, so that the plait ends can be concealed inside the purse.

Edging options

There are lots of different types of braid and other edgings that you can use to trim a medieval purse: narrow or tubular tablet weave, fingerloop braids, or even a nice twist, at a pinch. I don't have room to set up tablet weaving right now, and I hate doing fingerloop, so I am using some simple three-strand plaits made from Como silk.

Regarding fingerloop, fingerloop braids were commonly used in the Middles Ages to create short lengths of cord. Five loops of thread are tied together and the loops are distributed across the fingers of one hand to be looped into and out of each other – it is a bit like a more productive version of cat's cradle. I am not very good at it, and I find that it makes my fingers sore, but in the Further Reading list I have listed Elizabeth Benns' and Gina Barrett's excellent and well-researched book, *Tak V Bowes Departed*, that covers fifteenth-century braiding, for those of you who want to learn more.

28 The next step is to cover the whip stitching on the outside of the purse by using another plait or braid. In this case, you need to make sure that your braid is long enough to go around the three closed sides of the purse with at least twenty centimetres (about eight inches) to spare at each end.

To ensure even placement, measure the middle point of the braid, and attach that to the middle point of the bottom of the purse. All braids shift a little bit when you sew them down – they can expand or contract – and, if you sew from one end, its attachment is likely to come out uneven because of this. We want the extra bit of braid at each end to be even, so sew from the middle.

29 Separate the paired tassels so that one falls to each side of the braid.

Sew by sliding the needle through from side to side in a zigzag pattern that picks up the side of the braid, so ensure that the braid lies flat against the seam.

30 Once the braid is in place, you don't need to do anything else to the tassels: they should fall neatly along the sides of the purse.

31 Having stitched the braid up one side of the purse, loop it over and sew the end down inside the purse at the top, but leaving a loop from which the purse can later be hung. Attach the other half of the braid to the other side of the purse in the same manner. As with the braid covering the top seam between the embroidery and the silk cloth, this braid end can be concealed inside the purse lining.

32› Now, make a lining. You could use the same silk as used for the top, but I love a pretty lining, so I am using a scrap of reproduction thirteenth-century brocade left over from another project that was too gorgeous to waste.

Sew a simple bag, with right sides in; you can see for this purse that I have folded the brocade in half, to bring the two short sides together, and then sewn along the bottom edge and then up the open side. The lining bag needs to be taller than the purse so that you have room to turn the top, as shown, and I like to make it slightly wider as well – it will sit perfectly if you have to put a small pleat in, but, if you make it too small, it will never be right, so it is safest to err on the side of generosity.

I have machined my lining because the silk is prone to fray; if you hand sew, it is best to use a reinforced seam such as flat-felled or French.

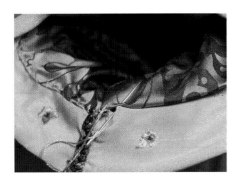

33 Whip stitch your lining into place, taking care to conceal the ends of the edging braids as you do so.

‹**34** The next step is to make and insert the drawstrings, in this case, we are using two more three-strand plaits, to be laced from opposite sides of the purse (as you can see, my braids are of slightly different widths). Note that each of the drawstrings should be twenty to thirty centimetres (about eight to twelve inches) longer than the circumference of the purse, or, in other words, twice the top width of the purse plus, again, twenty to thirty centimetres (about eight to twelve inches). Basically, they need to be long enough to go around the purse with a dangly bit to spare!

Using two drawstrings not only makes opening and closing the purse easier but also gives you symmetry and an excuse for even more tassels. It can take a little persuading to get the drawstrings through the holes; I like to poke the ends through with my stiletto, but it is a job that you have to do only once, as the drawstrings will be sealed to the purse and never taken out again.

I usually start at the middle of each drawstring when lacing, because you want the drawstring loop that crosses the side seam of the purse to go around the outside of the purse. If these loops cross on the inside of the purse, the drawstrings won't do their job properly, so starting in the middle of each drawstring saves a lot of cursing and pulling out to start again.

With one side seam of the purse facing you, take one end of one drawstring and, from the outside, insert it into the nearest (first) hole on the right-hand side of the bag. Pull the drawstring through until the middle of the drawstring is in line with the side seam and the braid sits flat against the purse. Next, insert the other end of the drawstring into the nearest hole on the left-hand side of the bag, and pull through the slack of the drawstring until again the braid lies flats against the purse. From the inside of the purse, insert the end of the right-hand drawstring into the nearest (second) hole on the same side of the purse, and repeat for the left-hand drawstring. Keep inserting the end of the drawstring into the nearest hole along the same side of the purse until both drawstring ends emerge from the inside of the purse to the outside, on each side of the opposite side seam, with tails of an even length (because you made sure that the middle of the drawstring lined up with the first side seam).

Repeat this threading process for the other drawstring, by starting from the side seam where the first drawstring tails emerge: this way, you create a double lacing that will allow you to effectively close your purse.

‹**35** Make sure that the ends of each drawstring are pulled out evenly, to extend from the purse by the same amount. With the purse laid flat and the drawstrings relaxed, there should be at least eight to ten centimetres (about three to four inches) of braid to spare at each end.

Cross the braids towards their ends and then secure the crossing point with a couple of stitches, as shown.

36 Use the end of the sewing thread to wrap around and neatly cover the crossing point, then stitch underneath these wraps to secure the thread, just as with the heads of the tassels.

37 Take a pair of tassels and sew their suspension threads through one end of one drawstring braid. Do the same for the other three drawstring-braid ends. Here, I haven't cut my braid to the desired length yet: I will do that once each of the tassels are in place, so at this stage I have just sewn this pair of tassels where I want to drawstring end to be.

38 If you need to trim the braid, do it at the last minute to avoid fraying, then thread wrap the join between the tassels and the braid in the same way as before.

39 Your almoner's purse is finished; here you can see the Rapunzel-panel side.

40 And here you can see the Rumpelstiltskin-panel side.

FURTHER READING

It is not my intention to provide an exhaustive bibliography for opus anglicanum; rather, these are useful references for finding pictures of original pieces or manuscripts to use for inspiration. Please note that some titles are in another language, but they are still worth having for the illustrations.

Benns, E., and Barrett, G., *Tak V Bowes Departed, a 15th Century Braiding Manual Examined* (Soper Lane, 2006)

Bergemann, U-C. (ed.), Europäische Stickereien 1250–1650: Katalog des Deutschen Textilmuseums Krefeld Band 3 (Schnell& Steiner, 2010)

Boak, R., *Sacred Stitches: Ecclesiastical Textiles in the Rothschild Collection at Waddesdon Manor* (The Rothschild Foundation, 2013)

Browne, C., Davies, G., and Michael, M.A., *English Medieval Embroidery: Opus Anglicanum* (Yale University Press, 2016)

Dean, B., *Embroidery in Ritual and Ceremonial* (Batsford Ltd, 1981)

Descatoire, C., *L'Art en Broderie au Moyen Âge* (Musee du Cluny, 2019)

Freeman, M.B., *The St. Martin Embroideries* (Metropolitan Museum of Art, 1968)

Garrett, R., and Reeves, M., *Late-Medieval and Renaissance Textiles* (Sam Fogg, 2018)

Ivy, J., *Embroideries at Durham Cathedral* (Dean & Chapter of Durham, 1992). This is a cathedral guidebook; there is a more scholarly volume, but you will need access to an academic library to find and look at a copy.

Johnstone, P., *High Fashion in the Church, The Place of Church Vestments in the History of Art from the Ninth to the Nineteenth Century* (Maney Publishing, 2002)

King, D., *Opus Anglicanum, English Medieval Embroidery* (The Curwen Press, 1963)

King, D., and Levy, S., *Embroidery in Britain from 1200 to 1750* (Victoria and Albert Museum, 1993)

Michael, M.A. (ed.), *The Age of Opus Anglicanum* (Harvey Miller Publishers, 2016)

Staniland, K., *Embroiderers* (Medieval Craftsmen series) (British Museum Press, 1991)

Walther, I.F., and Siebert, G., *Codex Manesse: Die Miniaturen der Grossen Heidelberger Liederhandschrift* (Insel Verlag, 1988)

It is also worth mentioning the excellent journal *Medieval Clothing and Textiles*, published annually by Boydell and Brewer, which often features interesting scholarly articles about medieval embroidery.

SUPPLIERS

Wool and ramie fabrics, passing threads and kits

Tanya Bentham's website
https://www.opusanglicanumembroidery.com

Courses and inspiration

Tanya Bentham's blog
https://opusanglicanum.wordpress.com
Tanya Bentham's Instagram
https://www.instagram.com/opusanglicanum/

Smooth-passing threads

Benton & Johnson
Regalia House
Newtown Road
Bedworth
Warwickshire
CV12 8QR
https://toyekenningandspencer.co.uk/shop/benton-johnson.html
For product availability and information, please email Neil Halford at the address neil.halford@toye.com

Japan gold threads

Midori Matsushima
http://www.midori-embroidery.com

Silk-filament threads

DeVere Yarns
Weavers House
Hyde Wood Road
Little Yeldham
Halstead
Essex
CO9 4QX
https://www.devereyarns.co.uk

Silk threads, including tram silks

The Handweavers Studio & Gallery
140 Seven Sisters Road
London
N7 7NS
https://www.handweavers.co.uk

Silk threads

Pipers Silks
https://pipers-silks.com
Au Ver à Soie
http://www.silk-thread.com

Silk fabrics

Beckford Silk
Beckford
Near Tewkesbury
Gloucestershire
GL20 7AU
https://beckfordsilk.co.uk

Naturally dyed, twisted silk threads and linen threads

The Mulberry Dyer
https://mulberrydyer.com

Slate frames

Simon and Lesley Dunn
History in the Making
Old Post Office
Shore Road
Garthorpe
Scunthorpe
DN17 4AD
https://historyinthemaking.co.uk
mail@historyinthemaking.co.uk

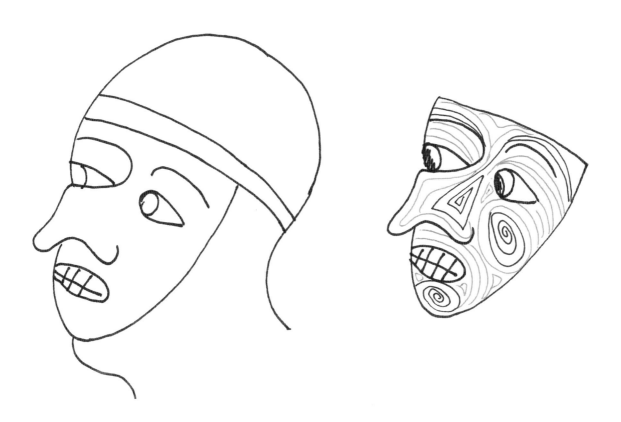

Enlarge 200%

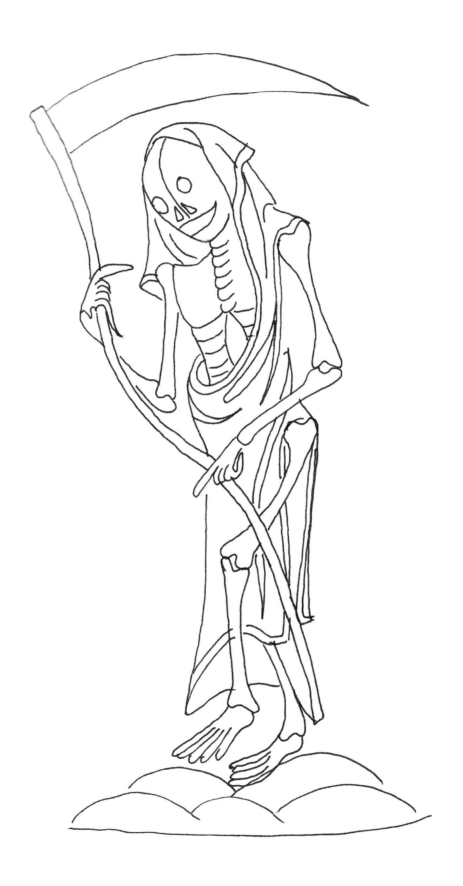

Enlarge 200%

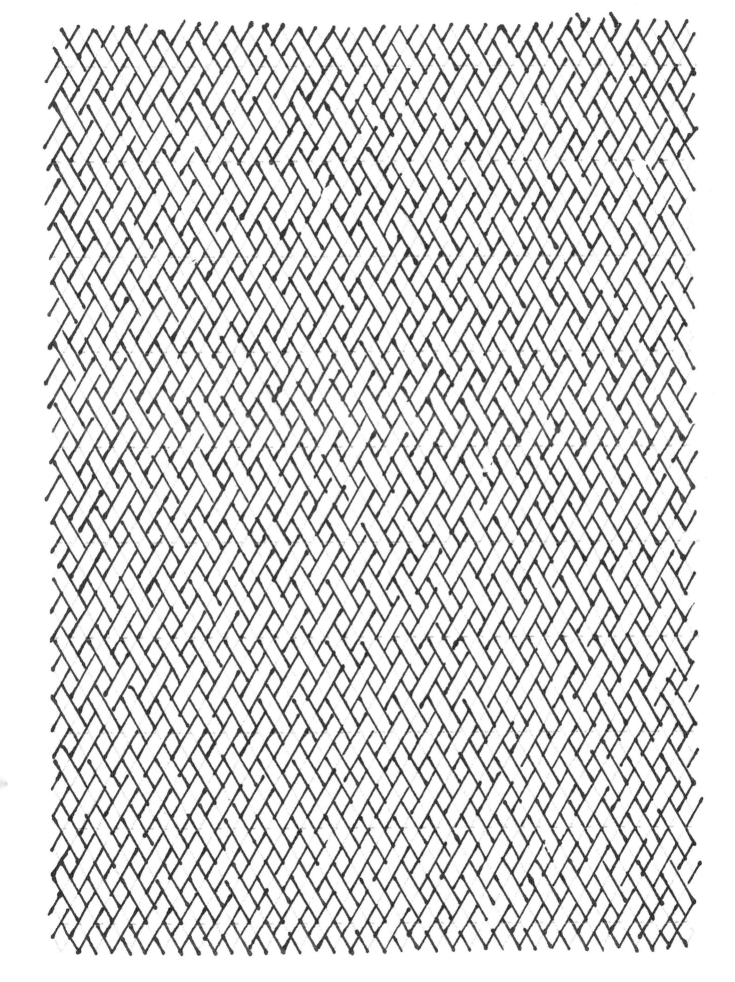

Enlarge 200%

Enlarge 200%

Enlarge 200%

INDEX